The ParenTalk Guide to Brothers and Sisters

The **Paren**talk Guide to Brothers and Sisters

Pat Spungin and Victoria Richardson

Series Editor: Steve Chalke

Illustrated by John Byrne

Hodder & Stoughton
LONDON SYDNEY AUCKLAND

British Library Cataloguing in Publication Data
A record for this book is available from the British Library

ISBN 0 340 8543 8

Typeset by Avon Dataset Ltd, Bidford-on-Avon, Warks

Printed and bound in Great Britain by
Clays Ltd, St Ives plc

Hodder and Stoughton
A Division of Hodder Headline Ltd
338 Euston Road
London NW1 3BH

Contents

Acknowledgements

My thanks to my children, Rachel, Joel and Hannah, for providing me with many examples of sibling love as well as of sibling rivalry. To my husband, Meir, my deep gratitude for his consistent support and for his many insights into family life. Finally I'd like to thank my own siblings, John and Liz, who can always be relied on – living proof that 'a brother or sister is for life'.

Pat Spungin

Thanks to my mum, Ellen Richardson, our Webmaster Andy and Interactivity Editor Camilla for all their hard work, assistance and limitless reserves of patience.

Victoria Richardson

Thanks also to all the visitors to raisingkids.co.uk who contributed their own experiences of sibling life, and finally, many thanks to Tim Mungeam and Maggie Doherty of Parentalk who have been so sympathetic and supportive of raisingkids.co.uk.

Blood Is Thicker than Water

Peace Has Broken Out

There they sit. A twelve-year-old boy and his ten-year-old sister. Cosy as an old married couple, watching television together and discussing the ins and outs of a new soap plot.

Yet ten minutes ago, just like an old married couple too, they were deep into one of their well-rehearsed squabbles about who should have the TV remote control. That problem has obviously been sorted to their satisfaction and normal relations have resumed.

Sibling Fact

Most children grow up in the company of brothers and sisters. The typical four- to five-year-old child spends twice as much time with his siblings as with his mother.

What a complex relationship they have – and what a lot they are learning from each other. As I watch them, I think how little importance is placed on the relationship between brothers and sisters. It surprises me, since most children spend more time with their siblings than they do with their parents.

Most of what we read about this relationship is negative. Say 'sibling' and the next word is usually 'rivalry'. New baby? Oh dear! Isn't the older one going to be jealous?!

At the same time, we rarely seem to hear about the other side of the coin. About, for example, the nervous five-year-old standing in the playground in her first week at school, happier for the knowledge that big brother is keeping an eye out. Or the eight-year-old who is no longer scared of the dark now that he shares a bedroom with his big brother. Or the fifteen-year-old boys who thank their lucky stars they have sisters and aren't scared to talk to girls – unlike some of their mates!

'Let's Stick Together . . .'

My husband and I had dinner with our three children just recently. Since two are at university and one is working, this is a rare occurrence nowadays. We had a terrific time, laughing and joking and enjoying the family sport of teasing Dad.

Seeing the three of them together, my husband felt moved to make a little speech. 'I hope,' he said, 'you three won't lose touch with each other as you grow older. Blood is thicker than water, and whenever one of you needs help I hope you'll turn to each other and not become strangers.'

 Top Tip: Help your children build strong bonds with each other and they will last a lifetime.

The relationship between brothers and sisters isn't always harmonious – or even comfortable – but it's always there! In times of crisis, many people turn to their brother or sister first, even if they're not on particularly good terms with them. If, as they say, home is the place where 'when you have to go there, they have to let you in', then siblings are the people who 'when you have to turn to them, they have to lend a helping hand'.

What Brothers and Sisters Learn From Each Other

That's My Role Model!

From the kitchen window, I can see two-year-old Anita following older brother Ben around the garden. Whatever he does, she religiously copies. As he pushes his cars around and makes 'vroom-vroom' noises, she watches intently then pushes her car too. He gets up to examine something on a bush, she gets up too and looks just as carefully. Then he decides to pee against the garden fence. Well, you can't always copy everything big brother does!

I LIKE TO COPY MY OLDER BROTHER— LOOK... I JUST COPIED HIS PICTURE ON THE WALL!

Copying is how little children learn. If a big sister sits at the table and eats properly, cleans her own teeth and hangs her own coat up, then her little brother will want to do the same.

 Top Tip: *Use copying to encourage good habits in younger brothers and sisters.*

It's not only practical skills that little sibling learns from big sibling. A high percentage of the children who start school already knowing their letters and numbers learn them from their older siblings – usually while playing make-believe games of 'school'.

 Top Tip: *The best way for your kids to learn how to interact with other children is to start with their siblings.*

At the same time, there is another kind of learning going on between brothers and sisters. Psychologists call it *social learning*. They are learning how to deal with other people. All children learn how to relate to their parents, but it's only the kids with brothers and sisters who have an intensive course in how to get on with other children.

And it shows. When they start at school, children with siblings – especially the ones with older siblings – play together better, ask more questions and are generally more outgoing.

When you've got a sibling, there's nowhere to hide. You have to work it out somehow. Siblings teach each other six important skills:

Lesson One: Sharing

'It's Mine!!!'

One television, two children who want to watch different programmes.

They can – of course – fight it out, but the noise they make brings an adult, who switches the TV off. Now nobody gets to watch what they want. So, since the problem cannot be solved by force, a solution has to be found by agreement. That solution has to be fair to everyone or another fight will start. To reach a solution that makes everyone more or less happy, brothers and sisters have to learn how to share.

Learning to share means learning the art of give and take and the skill of negotiating. Younger siblings learn to stick up for themselves and to push for what they want. Older siblings learn that 'might is not always right' and that other people have rights that have to be taken into account.

In our house, a system of Byzantine complexity evolved around watching television together. Who should have the remote control? How long should they keep it? Could they use it during the adverts? If you had the remote, should you give up the best chair? NATO was unavailable to deal with this very important issue and my kids had to sort it out themselves.

Everyone Gets a Pizza the Action

Take the Pizza Question, which I saw in operation with my nephews. Their parents are going out and the boys are having takeaway pizza but have only been given a certain amount of money. Deciding what pizza to order with a limited budget calls for hard bargaining. What to choose? One likes Pizza Express while the other favours Domino's. Thin crust or thick crust? What kind of toppings?

An argument starts and is cut short by my brother saying, 'Sort it out or no pizza at all.' That concentrates minds, and within ten minutes the pizza is ordered and both are more or less satisfied. That's negotiation.

Share and Share Alike

Where would you learn to negotiate these things if you didn't have a brother or sister whose preferences you had to take into account? Singletons need to look outside the family to learn the skills of hard bargaining. They may have to share with friends when they visit but they can always go home. It's not the same cut-and-thrust as twenty-four-seven life with a brother or sister.

Lesson Two: Fairness

'It's Not Fair!'

An only child gets everything his parents have to give, and although he may compare it with what his friends get, there is no one with whom he compares day in and day out. Siblings compare all the time.

All parents know the mantra 'It's not fair...' followed by a whole variety of different statements. Some are serious complaints ('It's not fair, you love him more than you love me') and some are almost laughably trivial ('It's not fair, he has more cornflakes than me').

Ideally each child would like to get the lion's share of what is on offer, be it undivided attention, more chocolate, more pocket money, first choice... This is unlikely to be accepted by the others because ... taa-daa!! ... 'it's not fair'.

You Pays Your Money and You Takes Your Choice

Here comes the choice. The thought process runs something like this: 'I know that I can't have everything I want, when I want it ... I have to take into account what my brothers and sisters want ... *but* ... it's only fair they can't have everything they want either.' Eureka! This leads to careful scrutiny of what others are getting, so everyone gets their fair share.

When children grow out of insisting that they get special treatment, they move on to insisting that no one gets special treatment. Everyone should be treated exactly the same. What a refined sense of fairness children develop when they are looking to see whether 'the others' are getting more than they are.

The problem is, as any parent will testify, this isn't a once-and-for-all business. 'It's not fair!' is the daily cry of warring siblings. Don't be too eager to intervene. If children are left to themselves to find a fair solution, usually they can work something out.

> **Top Tip:** Don't be too eager to jump in and sort out every dispute: you'll often be surprised how quickly your children can work things out when left to their own devices.

Lesson Three: Share the Knowledge, Share the Fun

'Been There, Done That!'

An older brother or sister is a very useful thing to have when starting at a new school. An older sibling can tell the younger one how to behave in the playground ('Stay away from that corner, that's where the rough boys play'), what to wear (and what not to be seen dead in!), what kind of lunch box is acceptable, which teachers or pupils to look out for. A big brother or sister in the playground is invaluable when the school bully looms. Later on, teenagers with brothers or sisters of the opposite sex have a reserve of insider knowledge that gives them an advantage in the chat-up stakes.

Careering Ahead?

Younger siblings often take on some of the interests and attitudes of their older siblings. This can have an effect later in life on choice of career. My daughter is studying Mechanical Engineering at university. Was she influenced by the many occasions when she sat with her older brother, contentedly playing with Lego? Very possibly. Although it was more suited to his age than to hers, he helped her out whenever she got stuck, until she became as proficient as he was and didn't need his help any more.

One Is Fun ... but Two Is Better

Having a brother or sister you can chat to and play with makes it far less lonely at home. Playing side by side is better than playing alone. It's much more fun to go swimming with your brother or sister than with just your parents, who want you to do boring things like swim lengths or learn to dive properly. With your brothers and sisters you can play games and have a good time ... and learn to be a good swimmer at the same time.

Lesson Four: United We Stand

Sibling Power! The Antidote to Parent Power

As the saying goes, 'Children and their grandparents are natural allies. They share a common enemy.' When the only bargaining tool kids have is 'pester power', two, three or four are more powerful than one.

When it comes to lobbying parents for new bedtime rules, more pocket money, cable television or anything else they fancy, siblings in cahoots can be a formidable gang. So long as their demands are reasonable, (occasional) parental capitulation does wonders to encourage your children's team spirit!

Lesson Five: Looking After Each Other

'He Ain't Heavy, He's My Brother'

Children often show a great deal of care and affection for their siblings. When three-year-old Divya was feeling poorly, her seven-year-old brother Sanjay sat and read to her from his school reading book. Some words he didn't understand, many words she didn't understand and the tale was rather faltering. Obviously, the story wasn't important. The point was having big brother sitting close and cuddling up to her as he read, showing sympathy for a little sister not feeling well.

Siblings *Contra Mundum*

Family solidarity is a strong point between siblings. As many parents know, children who fight like cat and dog at home will defend each other to the hilt in the outside world.

Lesson Six: At Home with the Opposite Sex

The Worst Fear Is the Fear of the Unknown

Growing up with two sisters meant girls were never some mysterious exotic species to my son. He may have gone to a boys-only school, but he is far more likely to be relaxed with girls. When he has girlfriend trouble, he has two ready-made Agony Aunts in the form of his sisters. Their advice comes on excellent authority! And it's not just a one-way street; sometimes he's even been known to offer his sisters a bit of advice too!

And Now for the Bad News

'You Can Change Your Friends, but You're Stuck with Your Family'

Sharing your parents, sharing your space and toys, competing for attention – all that takes some getting used to. And not everyone is good at getting used to it. Sibling rivalry is a reality. It may ebb and flow as the children grow, and many siblings who were daggers drawn throughout their childhood become close confidants and good friends as adults.

But sometimes the jealousies can last through childhood and beyond. In some cases they become so severe they affect the whole household. Here's the first sentence of a letter which was featured on a newspaper problem page: 'My fifteen-year-old son has not conversed or made eye contact with my seventeen-year-old daughter for two years.'

Much is written about sibling rivalry and it's a big concern for many parents. It may be the reason you bought this book. It would be foolish not to recognise the fighting, pinching, telling tales, surreptitious needling, teasing and tormenting which are the everyday realities of sibling relationships.

Birds in Their Little Nests Agree? Some Hope!

So just when and how does healthy competition between siblings become deadly rivalry? Is in-fighting inevitable from the day that Mum and Dad bring home a new baby to share the family home? Is this the day the seeds of rivalry are sown? Or is it possible to handle that transition from idolised only child to friendly twosome?

Preparing for a New Arrival

How Does It Feel?

It's good to have a sibling but it's not always fun. Especially for the firstborn, it can be a bolt from the blue. There you are, the light of your parents' life, commanding all the attention they have to give, indulged, fussed over, listened to – and then out of the blue comes a noisy, dirty, demanding infant. Strange though it seems, they seem to like it as much as they like you. Sometimes (it seems) even more.

It can wee anywhere, even mess its nappies. It keeps your mum and dad up all night and they don't seem to mind. If you do the same, they get cross and tell you to behave like a big boy or girl. Now, is that fair?

Sibling Fact

Your eldest may feel he's the only child in the world whose parents could play such a rotten trick on him but he's definitely not alone! Seventy-eight per cent of families are made up of more than one child.

Move Over!

Sometimes we forget what a shock it must be to the firstborn to have to move over and share the limelight. My husband and I sat watching the video of our son's third birthday. I sat at a table in the garden with my parents and our two younger children. Three-year-old Tom and nine-month-old Alice are being encouraged to smile for the camera and are being generally fussed over by all the adults present.

Seven-year-old Tara comes out of the house. She doesn't come to the table but sits apart from the rest of us. She occasionally interjects into the conversation, once saying something nasty to Tom, and then seems to give up and goes inside. When my husband and I saw this video ten years later, both of us were upset. We didn't see at the time how taken up with the little ones we were.

It seems to us we didn't understand how difficult it must have been for Tara, a four-year-old just starting school, to move over and make way for a younger brother. We thought a four-year-old was a 'big girl' compared with the little ones and we overlooked the fact that she was only four (now I think she was still a baby herself!).

Top Tip: *Your toddler may seem very mature compared with the new baby, but she still wants to be babied herself.*

Never Underestimate the Upset a New Baby May Cause!

Some firstborns are devastated when a 'rival' turns up. Poet Fleur Adcock claims to have taken sixty-two years to get over the arrival of her little sister and says, 'My heart was broken when my sister was born.' A friend in his thirties recently told me, quite matter-of-factly, that the worst day of his life happened when he was four years old and his younger brother turned up: 'Everything was all right before then.'

Perhaps that all seems a bit melodramatic, but where parents see a second or third child as a natural and longed-for addition to the family, little children may take quite a different view. For the eldest especially, the idea of not being the focus of your attention may previously have never occurred to them.

'If Only There Was a Bigger Gap Between Them!'

There's a lot written about sibling rivalry. It isn't surprising when parents, faced with battling siblings, sometimes imagine it might have been better if they had waited and had a bigger gap, or had another child sooner and had a smaller gap!

Does the gap between siblings really make any difference? Research suggests that when brothers and sisters are between two and four years apart, there is more jealousy and conflict between them. This unfortunately is the age gap most families are likely to have.

Sibling Fact

Whether they like it or not, most children get a little brother or sister while they are still toddlers themselves. Twenty-seven months is the average age gap between pregnancies in Britain.

Most families have a two to four year age gap between siblings, but bigger gaps are becoming more common. More mums are having babies later and the conception rate for women in their late thirties has almost doubled in the past twenty-five years.

Very few parents will space their children according to the likelihood of there being sibling conflict. Spacing between children is usually determined by pressures the parents face at work and at home. It's not always possible to conceive a baby according to the date pencilled in your Filofax! An age spacing of under two years may be better than a slightly larger gap as far as sibling relationships are concerned, but then there's more work when dealing with toddler tantrums and a new baby.

 Top Tip: *It's not the age gap that counts – it's the way you treat it.*

Mind the Gap!

Siblings compare themselves with each other and argue about what's fair: 'He's got more than me,' 'Why do I have to go to bed earlier?' 'She's got more pocket money than me . . .' If siblings are very close in age – less than two years between them – they're treated in a very similar manner because they're about the same age, so disputes about whether the treatment is fair will arise less often. When there's a big age gap, it's obvious there are different needs – for example, a nine-year-old will stay up later than a two-year-old – so again there are fewer things to squabble over.

'Where Do I Stand?'

When their children are between two and four years apart, parents sometimes treat them as if they are the same age and at other times make a distinction between them on the basis of their age. Deal with this by having clear rules related to their age and applying these rules consistently. This will go some way to stopping the perennial cry of 'It's not fair!'

If the age gap is four years or more, there's such a difference between siblings no comparisons are made, though as they get older and the significance of the age gap diminishes there may be more friction between them.

 Top Tip: *Respect children's age differences – don't expect the same responsibility, behaviour or bedtime from different ages.*

Sometimes It's Hard to Be a Firstborn

A firstborn who has been an 'only child' stands at the centre of the family universe. Suddenly there's a new baby and your older child has to make space – and occasionally gets pushed out. From the parents' point of view, a walking, talking three- or four-year-old appears 'grown up' compared with a totally helpless baby. Parents may expect the older child to adjust easily and may not notice signs of displacement.

 Top Tip: *If your first child is still a toddler, don't overestimate their maturity. Though they may appear forceful, active and outgoing, make allowances and time for them.*

How Do I Prepare My Child for a New Sibling?

Many parents assume sibling rivalry is inevitable, but it doesn't have to happen. It's important you approach the issue carefully, as your child's relationship with their new sibling is influenced by their parents' attitude before the birth and during the months afterwards.

Most families have a second child during the firstborn's toddler years, but if your child is older (or even a teenager) don't assume their age will mean that they have less strong feelings about the arrival of a new sibling. Don't leave your older children to find out when you bring home the Mothercare bags.

One woman was fifteen when her younger brother was born, and now, even twenty years later, she remembers it:

I knew my dad had always wanted a son and I felt very, very jealous. David was born at home, but I wouldn't look at him for the first twenty-four hours. I was just coming into puberty and this was the first time anything had rocked my life.

MUM AND DAD ARE
EXPECTING A HAPPY
EVENT THAT I'M
NOT VERY HAPPY
ABOUT...

To Begin at the Beginning ... or Before the Beginning

Sometimes the problems begin – or seem to begin – even before the baby is born. After the initial euphoria of discovering that you're pregnant, the questions arise: what and when shall we tell the children?

To a large extent, this depends on the age of your existing children. When Anna got the news she was pregnant, she and husband Mike were delighted. They were both completely sure their four-year-old son Jack would also love the idea of a new little brother or sister.

When they mentioned it to Jack, however, he was distinctly underwhelmed. He flatly stated he didn't want a baby brother or sister and asked for a rabbit instead. Anna and Mike were upset and tried to persuade Jack that it would be really nice to have 'a new playmate', but Jack was having none of it. He didn't want a brother or sister and that was that!

'What's Worrying You?'

So what do you do if you're seven months pregnant and your child is adamant he doesn't want a new baby? The first thing is not to panic because your idea of happy families seems to have been dealt a body blow. Don't over-react and automatically assume you are looking at a lifetime of sibling rivalry. Check out precisely what it is your child is concerned about. It may have nothing at all to do with the expected baby.

It's unlikely four-year-old Jack really understood what a new baby would mean in terms of his mummy's time and affection. Jack was probably worried about practical things, like 'Will I have to give up my "baba" (his precious comfort blanket) to the new baby?' or 'Will they make me share my teddy with the baby?'

The most important thing is to listen. Your toddler will have trouble talking about their worries, so don't ask, 'Why don't you want a new baby?' It's not the sort of question a toddler can answer.

Show Them What to Expect

If some of your friends have small babies, take your toddler to visit the family, and afterwards talk about the baby. Your child's questions may reveal their worries. Anna took Jack to visit friends, who had a new baby. Afterwards Anna and Jack talked about the baby and, sure enough, most of his questions were about the baby's sleeping arrangements. Listen carefully to what your toddler says. Anna learned a lot from Jack's reactions when he asked, 'Where will our baby sleep?' and 'Do all babies sleep in a cot?' She realised he was worried he would have to give up his bed to the baby, because he hadn't seen anywhere at home where the baby could sleep. When she told him they were bringing out his old cot from the cupboard and the baby would sleep there, Jack was very relieved.

What if your child is absolutely, positively definite that they do not want a new baby? Don't expect them to love the baby just because you do, and don't go on trying to persuade them they will. Instead, help them express their feelings and deal with their questions, which are often just factual. Buy a book about having a baby brother or sister to read together. Talk about it and deal with any questions that come up.

An older child may worry about whether you'll still come to their school play, or even whether there'll be only half as many Christmas presents this year! They may be older but they will still be looking for reassurance.

 Top Tip: *Like adults, children often fear change, so emphasise that many things will stay the same after the baby's birth.*

It's important to prepare your child well for the birth of the baby, but be careful how you do it. Let her feel the baby moving or buy small things for the new baby, but don't make too much of a fuss or the older child may wonder what's so special and may even get to resent it. If you have photographs of yourself when pregnant with her, look at them together. Let her know her birth was also a cause for great excitement and rejoicing.

My five-year-old began to feel left out even before the baby was born. I worked so hard to get her to share in the excitement that I kind of overdid it. She couldn't really grasp the reality of the new baby but we kept going on and on about it. It was like something important was happening but she didn't really know what. I never noticed it but my mother pointed out that she was feeling left out. So one afternoon, I got out the photos of me when I was pregnant, pictures of her when she was very young and some of her baby clothes I was getting ready for the new baby. She was thrilled . . . and suddenly I think she felt part of it.

(courtesy: raisingkids.co.uk)

When Should You Tell?

Ever been in a car with children on your way to a summer holiday? Five minutes away from home and the chorus line 'Are we there yet?' is repeated every few minutes. The concept of time to a toddler is entirely different to an adult's, and so there's little chance that you'll avoid the mantra 'Is the baby coming yet?' Nine months may seem a short time to you but it's more than a third of a two-year-old's lifetime!

Some parents prefer to wait until the end of the uncertain first three months before telling their child about a new baby, but do it as soon as you feel comfortable. You'll probably want to give your child the opportunity to get excited with you about the baby, and allowing them to ask all the questions they want to, feel the baby, etc., will limit the number of surprises that they have to cope with when the time comes.

Bear in mind, though, that with the typical age gap between siblings somewhere between twenty-four and forty-two months, your eldest (but still young) child will need a fuller explanation (and reassurance) about what *exactly* is going to happen as the time draws closer.

Obviously, an older child can cope with more advance warning. One thing to note: if your pregnancy is complicated and there's a possibility you'll be taken into hospital at short notice, then it's better to give your kids, especially older ones, more notice.

I Heard It Through the Grapevine

Your three-year-old's going to get a shock if the first they hear about it is when a well-meaning auntie or uncle asks them if they're excited about the new baby. Timing is even more important with a bigger age difference.

One seventeen-year-old heard her mum was pregnant when her friend saw her mum looking at baby things in Baby Gap. With second marriages becoming very common, the difference between children of the first marriage and those of the second can often be fifteen or more years. Don't assume that because he appears to be grown up your teenager will accept the news without comment.

Teenagers, who are dealing with their own personal crises, need their parents more than they admit. The prospect of a demanding baby in the house (instead of a demanding teenager) will not appeal. Their own budding sexuality may make them feel embarrassed at the evidence their parents have 'done it' – *eeuuuch!* As the daughter of my forty-year-old friend said, 'But you can't be, you're too old!'

When breaking the news to teenagers, keep a sense of humour! It helps keep the tension down and gives them a useful cover to hide their own initial shock or embarrassment.

If the new baby is a stepsibling, an older child may even want to spend some time with their other parent for a while. Try not to feel rejected – they may just need some time to think. Take your lead from your teenager and let him deal with his feelings alone for a while, if that's what he wants.

'I'd Rather Have a Rabbit!'

One mum of our acquaintance, thrilled to be expecting Baby Number Four, sat her children down and told them there was going to be a 'lovely surprise'. Full of expectation and anticipation they listened eagerly, but when she told them she was expecting a new baby her seven-year-old burst into tears. He'd expected her to say they were going to go to Disneyland!

Other common reactions are to ask for a pet instead. Or to ask why they weren't directly involved in the process of getting the new baby . . . When one six-year-old heard she was going to have a new sister or brother, she asked her parents why they hadn't called her to see Daddy putting the 'pip' in!

Be Realistic and Honest

What should you say about the new baby? Prepare your older child in a matter-of-fact and honest way. Refer to friends who have younger brothers and sisters and tell your child they will be a big brother or sister soon.

Trying to prepare the older child for the arrival of the new baby, many parents go into overdrive and paint an exciting picture of what it will be like when the new baby arrives. 'Won't it be wonderful!' they say. 'You'll have a little playmate.' Oh no they won't! They will have a boring unappealing blob that doesn't talk, can't play and takes up an inordinate amount of parental attention. Tell the truth – the baby will mostly sleep, eat and cry and, in the beginning, will make Mummy tired.

Most important, prepare your older child for the delivery by explaining you'll be going away to hospital when the baby's ready to come, and make it clear who will look after them while you're there. Be sure your toddler understands you'll be coming back afterwards!

Talk about *Our* Baby

Involve your child in your preparations by getting her to help choose the decorations for the room or sort out the baby things. Show her ultrasound pictures of her new brother or sister. If you've chosen to know whether the new baby will be a boy or girl, call the baby 'he' or 'she' rather than 'it'! If you're one

27

hundred per cent sure in advance what the baby's name will be, encourage your child to use it. This all helps to make it more real.

Don't Go Changing!

Stick to familiar routines. The arrival of a new sibling may not be a problem but it will be a disruption. It can be difficult for your child to adjust to a new sibling, as indeed it is for you to adjust to becoming the parents of two children rather than just one. Since children dislike change and disturbances in their world, one major change is enough. Therefore keep everything else as much the same as is possible.

If you want your child to move to another bedroom, do it well in advance of the birth. If you've always watched a video together before bed, keep the routine going. Make sure your eldest is well settled into her new playgroup, or any other activity outside the home, before the new baby arrives, so it doesn't look as if she's been pushed out of the home to make way for the new baby. Try to keep daily life as routine as possible.

Top Tip: Pay attention to the details as well as the big picture.

Though most parents appreciate the need to keep the big things the same, they sometimes overlook the importance of little things. Avoid giving the new baby the baby toys or blankets discarded by the older sibling without asking first, especially if they are only recently outgrown. Things may seem trivial to you but may be significant to your child.

Happy Birth Day

In the UK, 98 per cent of mums have their babies in hospital. If this is what you intend to do, make sure your older child knows what's happening and when you'll be home. Leave them with someone they know well and are already used to. When in hospital, make sure you give your older child your attention, as visitors tend to concentrate almost exclusively on the baby. Don't be tempted to do too much showing off of the new baby, at least not in front of your older child.

 Top Tip: Remember, your child wants to visit YOU in hospital, not the wailing prune in the cot!

Home Birth
An increasing number of mums opt for a home birth and some choose to have their older children present. Will your older child – or children – be present in the room during your labour? During the birth itself? Either way, it's essential to be well prepared.

If you intend them to be present, in late pregnancy talk about how babies are born. Show pictures of births and of newborn

29

babies, showing how wrinkly and red they are. Act out the birth, making the noises you are likely to make at the time. This way your child won't get a shock when they hear you breathing loudly and yelling in pain.

Labour is a long process, so make sure there are other things for your child to do when they get tired of waiting. During the labour itself, have a friend or grandparent on hand whose top priority is looking after your older child or children. If there are complications with the delivery, then it's best to take the children from the room and occupy them elsewhere.

Home at Last!

Getting Off to a Good Start

Bringing home a new baby is often compared to introducing a new girlfriend into the home. Imagine your partner brought home a new girlfriend and told you she was coming to live with you, but things wouldn't change and he would still love you as much as ever. How would you feel? Come to think of it, how would he feel when he picked himself up off the floor!

So now imagine how your child feels when you bring home a new baby. The vision of happy families you might have had may recede a little as your child begins to feel pushed out and neglected.

Sometimes things don't go entirely to plan:

My children are only thirteen months apart and we were hopeful we wouldn't have too many problems when Number

Two Son came along, having spent months talking about 'the new baby in Mummy's tummy'. How wrong I was! From the moment I came home from hospital, my eldest cried for three solid weeks. Each morning he'd come downstairs in a good mood and then, the moment he saw his brother, he'd erupt into tears. He'd obviously forgotten about him overnight. For the next few weeks, he'd keep lifting my jumper and looking to see if there were any more to come out!

(courtesy: raisingkids.co.uk)

'Why Isn't One of Me Enough?'

You're excited about the new baby. Everyone is making the greatest fuss. Your older child may wonder why you wanted another one. Wasn't she cute, well-behaved or special enough for you?

> **Top Tip:** Coming home is a critical time for paying attention – not to your new baby but to your older child.

A few months ago, I went to a christening and, afterwards, to the home of the proud parents. The house was full of aunts and uncles, grandparents and friends, cooing and fussing over the new baby. On a table there was a pile of christening presents for the baby. As his mother sat with the baby, the three-year-old firstborn tried to push himself on to his mother's lap instead of the baby. She called over his dad to take him away but, furious, the older child threw a major tantrum.

Speak to your friends and relatives, and ask them, if they're bringing a present for the baby, whether they can perhaps also bring something small to congratulate the 'big brother' or 'big sister'.

Mummy's Little Helper

There's nothing worse than standing on the sidelines, especially if you've been used to standing centre stage. This is how your toddler may feel. You used to do everything together and now you spend such a lot of time with the baby. Enlist the help of your older child in taking care of your new baby. A toddler can choose the baby's clothes, bring soap and creams for the bath and generally be helpful to you. Thank him for helping you, and while looking after the physical needs of the baby keep up a conversation with your older child. All he wants is to be a part of it all!

Top Tip: Feed your baby... talk to your older child!

Remember to Take Care of Yourself, Too!

Don't forget you're going to be tired as well. The demands of a new baby plus giving extra attention to your other child – or children – can leave you worn out. Prepare for this as much as you can and get as much help as possible from friends and relations. Don't be afraid to ask.

Top Tip: Most friends and family will be happy to help out – so just ask!

If you're exhausted and tetchy and your new baby takes up a lot of your time, make sure you and your partner make a special time for your older child... and also for each other.

A school-age child may appear to be adjusting well to the arrival of the new infant, but watch carefully to see how your five- or six-year-old is reacting. He may not throw a tantrum but that doesn't mean he's not affected. It's a good idea to explain the situation to his teacher – who will probably have seen all this before – and ask them to keep an eye out.

Actions Speak Louder than Words

Don't anticipate jealousy or say things like 'Don't be silly, of course we still love you!' If you say, 'Mummy and Daddy will still love you when the new baby is born,' you could introduce a worry your toddler has never even considered! If your little one seems insecure, reassure her with affection and attention rather than words.

Newborns need a lot of feeding, bathing and changing, but they don't talk a lot. Your toddler, by contrast, is quite independent – but, boy, does he love to talk! So while you are looking after the baby's physical needs, you and your toddler can be chatting, singing and joking.

 Top Tip: *Show, don't say. It's your presence – not your presents – that's important.*

The most important thing you can give your older child is your attention. It's easy to cut down on the time you used to have with your older child when the baby's demanding and you're worn out. Try to make a time each day which is 'special time' with your older child.

35

It's Not the Baby's Fault

Avoid making the baby an excuse for not doing things together. Don't say things like 'We can't go to the park now because it's the baby's feed time,' or 'Don't make so much noise! The baby's sleeping.' Your little one will come to feel that the baby's spoiling his fun. Well, wouldn't you? It's better to say things like 'Shall we go to the park after lunch?' or, when you could do with some peace, 'Let's have a quiet read together now, shall we?'

 Top Tip: *Though it may be the case that the new baby stops you doing things with your older child, try not to make the baby an excuse for not doing things together.*

Regression: One Step Forward, Three Steps Back

A very common reaction to the birth of a new sibling is when the older child reverts to old 'baby ways'. This is especially true when the older sibling is too young to express her feelings in words. Psychologists call this *regression*. Common symptoms are bed-wetting, tantrums, refusal to get on with toilet training, wanting to be breastfed or pushing the baby off your lap. You may notice it particularly at the end of the day when your toddler is tired.

Take a child's-eye view of what is going on. After all, the new baby cries all the time, isn't potty-trained and can't feed itself, but it sure gets a lot of attention! It certainly looks as if being a baby is better than being a big girl or boy. So your child goes back to being a baby. Have patience and accept this is perfectly normal behaviour. A few weeks and everyone will have settled down to where they were before, including your toddler. Just have a little patience.

If you don't believe me, this eldest son is now at university and definitely doesn't want to sleep in a cot any more!

Despite the fact his parents had bought him a brand-new bed, when the new baby came Jamie wanted to go back to his old cot. His parents decided not to make an issue of it, and let him sleep there until he had accepted the baby and was ready to give up the cot of his own accord.

WHAT WILL WE DO ABOUT REGRESSION TO BABY BEHAVIOUR ONCE THE NEWBORN ARRIVES?

WE'LL COPE... BUT TRY NOT TO DO IT TOO MUCH.

A Change of Heart?
'I don't like the baby any more, take it back now!'

If everything's been going smoothly for the first few weeks, you may be nursing the idea that with another child your family is now complete, a perfect little family group. Then your older child drives a coach and horses through this fantasy by telling you she doesn't like the baby and she wants you to take the baby back!

My friend Jane's experience is very typical. When she brought home baby Chloe, three-year-old Rebecca was thrilled. She rushed around helping and proudly showed all the baby's new toys and clothes to visiting relatives and friends. Jane was very relieved everything was going so well . . . and then the trouble started. Rebecca, who had been dry at night for months, started to wet the bed. When Jane was nursing the baby, Rebecca would start to act up and be very naughty.

What to Do about Regression

It's not hard to see things as Rebecca saw them. The new baby does all kinds of things she was encouraged to give up, like crying all night and wetting himself, so naturally she thinks it's a good idea to do the same. Give attention to the 'grown-up' things she can do and let her take pride in being able to do lots of things the baby is too young to manage.

 Top Tip: *Peeing in the toilet may not seem a big deal to you, but it's one of your toddler's biggest achievements to date! Don't let it go unnoticed.*

Don't Tell Them to 'Grow Up'!

Don't urge your toddler to be a 'big' girl or boy – it's counter-productive. They don't want to be 'the big one', they want to be the limelight-stealing baby. If you criticise babyish behaviour outright, your child may feel any lapses or backsliding on her part make her unlovable.

Jane ignored Rebecca's bed-wetting but made a big fuss of her when the bed was dry in the morning. During the day she made an effort to spend more time with Rebecca, and after two or three weeks Rebecca settled down and went back to being dry at night.

'Who Brought That Baby Here?'

Sometimes the firstborn identifies the real culprits . . .

When they had their third baby, Mike and Sue were prepared for their middle child – who was still a toddler – to show some classic signs of sibling rivalry. They'd seen it before when their second child had been born, they'd played it according to the book, and slowly things had got better. They expected three-year-old Gareth to ignore the baby or to ask them to take her back, but what they didn't expect was his angry behaviour towards *them*. Gareth seemed to like the baby but he was definitely furious with them.

Gareth's point of view was clear. The baby wasn't to blame; after all, she didn't ask to be born. As Gareth saw it, his parents were the ones who brought the baby into the house, they were the ones who had less time for him and it was they who gave far too much attention to the interloper. Once upon a time he had his mummy all to himself while his older brother was at nursery school. Now he had to share.

He wanted the attention he used to have. He wanted to chat, sing, joke, fool around, go to the park and all the rest – whatever he used to do before the new baby came.

I KNOW BABY'S HERE BECAUSE OF THE BIRDS AND BEES... BUT HOW COME IT'S ME THAT GOT STUNG?

It's Okay to be Angry

Feeling angry with a powerful parent can be a frightening thing for a small child, so make sure your toddler knows he is still special to you. Your child may be afraid her strong feelings will cause you to be angry with – or even reject – her, especially now there's a new baby on the scene.

Sue reassured Gareth that she understood his feelings and that it was okay to be angry. In a calm voice, she told Gareth that she realised he was angry with her and Daddy for spending so much time with the baby. At the same time, she also reassured him he was very special to her.

Then she set about doing things that included Gareth. She made a special time for him each afternoon, while the baby was asleep. Sometimes they sang together to the baby. She told him what she was doing, about how she had done the same things for him, and within a few days Gareth became his old self again.

'Big' brothers and sisters often need time to accept the presence of another child who makes demands on their parents, so make a space in your day when they can enjoy your undivided attention, and stick to it.

What Not to Say

Don't try to make your older child feel better by saying negative things about the baby. It'll damage their relationship in the future. In time, your older child will come to accept their sibling, and if you make negative comments now it sets a bad example.

Top Tip: *When you sling mud, you lose ground. So don't put the baby down to make your eldest feel good.*

Don't Say You Love Them More Than the Baby

Comparisons in love are always to be avoided. If you indicate you measure your love, your child will always be looking for indications as to which one you love most. The important thing for you is to recognise and value the uniqueness of each of your children and love each for who they are.

Top Tip: *Never compare your children – either favourably or unfavourably.*

And If Your Firstborn's not a Toddler?

An older child may appear to be adjusting well to the arrival of the new infant but you will be tired and the baby will take up a lot of your time. Whatever their age, your older child will miss your undivided attention. It even happens in the corridors of power – look, for example, at 'big brother' Euan Blair's drunken escapade, shortly after his little brother Leo arrived. Possibly coincidental, but possibly not. Your teen or pre-teen's attention-seeking may not make national news, but be on the lookout! Watch carefully for signs they are feeling left out. Make sure you put aside special time for them.

It Might Be Much Better Than You Think

A deep bond often develops between siblings with a big difference in ages. The large age difference often means less sibling rivalry than between 'conventionally spaced' brothers and sisters. If your firstborn is a teenager, look on the plus side. Girls are becoming maternal at this age, and even boys are developing a soft spot for little kids – teenagers often end up secretly excited and proud at their new 'big brother' or 'big sister' status.

Top Tip: *A new sibling can help an adolescent who's being difficult, because they often find themselves giving a lot of attention to the new child.*

If your teen or pre-teen begins 'regressing' – declining grades at school, a refusal to 'act their age' by helping with chores, or simply by being whiney and demanding – do exactly the same as you would with a toddler. Your 'big kid' wants your attention, and lots of it!

Sibling Fact

This may not be any consolation to a disgruntled older sib but the likelihood of having a brother or sister is falling. The average British woman will have 1.7 children.

(1999 National Statistics)

Squabbling and Fighting, Scratching and Biting

Siblings Squabble: Fact!

'I don't have any siblings,' said Hawkeye Pearce in M*A*S*H. 'My parents never sibbled.'

His parents had a quieter life as a consequence. In the words of the old joke, 99 per cent of brothers and sisters quarrel and the other 1 per cent are lying.

Siblings squabble and argue and complain. When they really get mad, they hit each other. With sharp-tongued siblings, teasing and name-calling are preferred weapons. Younger brothers and sisters become expert practitioners of the plaintive wail, certain to bring a concerned adult running to defend the poor little thing.

As Tom Jones Would Say . . .

You want the good news? It's not unusual. In fact, squabbling is perfectly normal. The bad news, however, is that your 'perfectly normal' kids will fight over everything and anything, and they probably won't stop until one of them leaves home! All siblings fight from time to time, and some siblings seem to fight all of the time.

Unfortunately, this book can't offer an instant magic formula for stopping sibling squabbles. The only guaranteed way of preventing sibling squabbles is to have one child! What it can do, however, is help you understand why they fight and give you some useful tools for damage-limitation.

How to Deal with Squabbles

There's an old Irish proverb which says, 'Better be quarrelling than lonesome', so when your children squabble try to keep a sense of perspective. A certain degree of squabbling is the sign of a healthy relationship.

A few years ago, I came across a family with two teenage children who hadn't spoken to each other for six months. The most interaction the daughter would have with her brother was to politely ask him to pass the salt or the potatoes at dinner. The rest of the time she would walk out of the room to avoid him and refuse to reply if he tried to start a conversation. Their parents were upset by all of this. But the thing that made them realise it was time for professional help was that their son couldn't even provoke his sister into an argument.

Top Tip: *If your children are always arguing it may not be the best way to communicate but at least they are still communicating with each other.*

The $64,000 Question

Why *do* they fight *all* the time? Just like adults, children feel angry or frustrated when they can't get their own way. Unlike adults, they haven't yet learned to channel that aggression in acceptable ways. What they do learn, and pretty quickly, is that it doesn't do to be aggressive with everyone in the family. If Mum or Dad won't let you have your own way then there's not much choice, you have to accept it. After all, they're bigger, stronger, they can stop your pocket money or forbid you to watch TV.

But when it's your brother or sister (probably only a few years older or younger) who's thwarting you, then there's a fighting chance of getting your way by using force.

Most squabbling is harmless and irritating rather than life-threatening. The main objectives of parents are to keep the noise down, stop them hurting each other and then to help them find ways to resolve problems amicably and work towards longer-term solutions. The reasons for sibling squabbles vary from day to day and hour to hour. Below are some of the main reasons and an indication of how to spot them.

1 It's Just Horseplay!

How to Spot It

You can generally identify this kind of fun fighting by the THUMP! CRASH! OWWW!!! noises. Horseplay is like one of those dust-cloud scraps in the *Beano* comic with full sound effects, and often includes giggling.

Walking through the hotel gardens on a recent holiday, we heard a massive rumpus in the undergrowth. Out of nowhere, a dozen monkeys shot out of the bushes and started running up trees, chasing each other, chattering excitedly and egging each other on. They were obviously playing a simian version of Tag and enjoying themselves hugely. If they hadn't been covered in fur, they would've been indistinguishable from children in an adventure playground.

Watch puppies, bear cubs or baby monkeys – any young mammals – playing together: they seem to love rough-and-tumble play. Human young are no different.

As we watched, one young monkey pointed at another and chattered something in his direction. Whatever this was, it couldn't have been very complimentary as a play fight immediately ensued. Exactly like children!

In our household, when our kids were small, Saturday morning was regularly enlivened by shouting and yelling and occasional bumps as our three children took over our double bed and played 'wrestling'. They used to wrestle each other on the bed until one was pushed off on to the floor. They made a lot of noise and sometimes somebody would yell because he or she had taken a bash, but they always had a great time.

Rough-and-tumble play is harmless fun and generally nobody gets hurt. Kids love it! Boys in particular enjoy this kind of play, but girls like to join in too. If the noise drives you crazy, find yourself a quiet place or send them off to play somewhere else.

With horseplay, unless you think they're likely to hurt themselves, let them get on with it.

Beware of Cover-Up Jobs

Rough-and-tumble is fine if nobody gets hurt, but sometimes things are not quite as they seem. A friend told me that when he was a child, his older brother had consistently bullied him under the guise of play fighting. Parents may dismiss it as just fun, but to the poor child who is getting hammered it's anything but!

> He would start to fight with me – just horseplay – but there would always be a point at which he really hurt me, by twisting my arm or pushing me to the floor. When my parents saw it they probably thought 'boys will be boys' and we were just playing around. They never asked me if I liked it and they never told my brother to stop hurting me, though sometimes they said to keep the noise down. If I protested, 'He's hurting me!' my brother would say 'I'm only fooling.' They made him stop, but only till the next time.
>
> (courtesy: raisingkids.co.uk)

Stamp out bullying as soon as you see it. Be ready to step in if fighting gets bitter, intense or violent.

 Top Tip: If you're not sure if it's play fighting or real fighting, check it out by asking, 'Is this a play fight or is it real?' If it's real for one child, stop it.

---

2 Tired and Tetchy

How to Spot It

Whingey and whiney, that's how kids are when they start this kind of squabble. Often it comes on at the end of a long day or a long journey. The fight usually starts over something your children wouldn't bat an eyelid over if they were feeling bright-eyed and bushy-tailed.

Cabin Fever and Sunday Blues

I read an interesting, if somewhat depressing, fact the other day – that there are more suicides on Sunday than any other day of the week. I wouldn't be surprised if there were more murders, too. In our house we made it a golden rule always to do something active with the children on Sunday. However wet, cold or damp, we would always go out on Sundays. Otherwise there would be shouting and screaming at the end of the day . . . and that's just the parents! We called it the Sunday Blues.

Others call it 'cabin fever'. It's the effect of being cooped up in a small space with other people for a long time. Too much time inside and too much time together without an outlet for their energies, and the play fights turn into real fights. Everybody ends up with frayed nerves.

Top Tip: *If your kids are becoming bad-tempered, whatever the weather get out of the house for a while.*

Days of the week and times of the day all have an impact on emotional climate. Some people get tense and irritable when they're tired, others are unbearable if they are hungry. Some people are just not 'morning people'. Talk to them within an hour of waking and they're barely civilised, but later in the day they're as sweet as can be.

'Leave Me Alone, I've Had a Bad Day'

A bad day at school, just like a bad day at the office, leaves children feeling frazzled, and ordinary irritations become material for a fight.

A little bit of forward planning can help avoid these squabbles. If your children fight more at the end of a busy school day, plan evening activities to help them wind down. Reading, listening to a story or watching television – avoiding violent and aggressive programmes – are all suitable low-key activities. If your daughter (like mine) hates the mornings, let the whole family give her a wide berth until closer to lunchtime.

3 Attention-Seeking

How to Spot It

The big giveaway for this kind of fighting is that they only do it when you're there! And they do it with one eye in your direction, watching for your reaction all the time. Sometimes the motive underlying this kind of fighting is to get the other sibling into trouble. Picking a fight often occurs when one or both are a bit bored, because it's certain to produce some excitement when parents get involved.

Are You Paying Attention?

A mum and her two young sons are on the train. Mum's reading her magazine and the boys have books, pencils and paper. The boys get bored and try engaging her in conversation but she's engrossed in her magazine. The boys turn their attention to each other and – with an eye on Mum – they begin to needle each other, until the younger one yells, 'Mummy! He pinched me!'

Irritated, she looks up, puts down her magazine with a sigh and gives them her full attention.

If your kids are fighting to get your attention, removing yourself from the scene should be enough to stop it. Make sure no one is likely to get hurt in your absence. Separate them if you can't stand the noise. Don't get involved and don't listen to their cries of 'It's not my fault!' or 'He started it!' – in that direction, madness lies. Just go to another room and put the television on loud. Making allowances for their ages, they should respect a parent's right to a bit of peace and quiet sometimes!

Top Tip: *Remember – just because they're seeking attention, it doesn't mean that you always have to give it to them.*

4 Bossing, Ordering and Telling

How to Spot It

Trigger phrases for this kind of a fight are 'Do that!' followed by 'No, why should I?' – and they're off. Sooner or later the phrases 'You're not the boss!' and 'You can't tell me what to do!' will also be heard.

At five-year-old Kim's birthday party, his older sister Teo is corralling the children most effectively and organising Pass the Parcel. Like a field marshal, she's issuing orders and bossing the younger ones around. Meekly, they follow her instructions. After all, she's a 'big girl'. The time will come, however, when 'Little Miss Bossy' (as she's known in the family) will find the three-year-gap between her and her younger sibling no longer confers the same authority. That's when battles begin.

'I'll be the Leader, I'm the Oldest!'

Older children come to assume certain rights because of their age. Your eldest may like to boss your younger child and be the leader at everything. An easy-going younger sibling may accept bossiness, especially if there's a large age gap. With a small age gap or a more assertive child, the older child's supremacy will be challenged, sometimes with fists.

You and your partner can try to pre-empt this by encouraging the older child to be more diplomatic in dealing with their young siblings. Explain that of course the little one will resist if they are bossed about and told what to do. Teach your own Little Miss (or Mr) Bossy gentler methods of getting younger brothers and sisters to co-operate.

5 Sharing and Possessions

How to Spot It

Battles over shared objects are probably the most common cause of fights between brothers and sisters. Key phrases are 'Gimme that!' 'It's mine!' 'I had it first!' Even when objects are not shared but the property of one child, they still cause rows when they are 'borrowed' or 'just looked at'.

'It's Mine! I Had It First!'

Three-year-old Scott is playing with bricks. Four-year-old Nathan comes wandering up and tries to join in. Furious, Scott tries to gather all the bricks in his arms so Nathan won't have anything to play with. Nathan picks up the ones that drop and Scott tries to grab them back. Typical toddler behaviour!

Fast forward. Fourteen-year-old Scott and fifteen-year-old Nathan are watching television. As the programme they are watching together finishes, Nathan flicks to MTV. 'I don't want to watch that, I want to watch the Formula One,' protests Scott, making a grab for the remote control. He switches to the motor racing. Nathan jumps up, goes to the television, changes the channel back to MTV and stands with his arms outstretched in front of the set. Typical teenage behaviour!

 Top Tip: *Encourage your children to negotiate, take turns and compromise.*

Share and Share Alike

Does this situation sound familiar?

'I wanna go on the computer!'
'Wait till I've finished . . .'
'Oi! You've started another game.'
'No I haven't! You made me mess up the last game because you interrupted me.'
'No I didn't. Gimme my go! Now!'
'Look, you've made me mess it up. I'll have to start over again now.'
'No, it's *my* turn now. You're horrible!'
WHACK.
'Ouch. Mu-u-u-m-m . . .'

It's rarely just about straightforward ownership. Some things are communal property – for example, the bathroom, the phone, the computer and television. Sharing these things means compromise and negotiation. Unless some system of sharing is worked out, there'll be clashes and fights over who uses what and when.

Learning to Play Co-operatively Takes Time

If your kids fight about who uses the computer and for how long, insist they work out a system of sharing or you won't allow either of them computer time. The same thing applies to the remote control. If one starts flicking from station to station when the others are getting interested in a programme, then there is bound to be trouble. Again, the best method is usually to insist they work out a solution for themselves, with the threat that if they don't no one will be allowed to watch.

 Top Tip: *Teach your children to respect each other's possessions but also to be willing to share some things.*

Learning to share also takes time, and there are some precious objects that none of us want to share. Parents like their children to be generous and occasionally try to force sharing on a reluctant child. This isn't always a good idea. You can't force generosity, especially if the object is very precious. You have to take into account the possibility that it might be damaged, especially if younger children are involved.

Taking and 'Borrowing'

Here's a typical exchange about taking and borrowing.

'That's my necklace you're wearing!'

'So? I've just borrowed it. You're not wearing it at the moment anyway.'

'I don't care. It's mine. Take it off!'

'You're so-o-o selfish. I would let you borrow it if it was mine.'

'No you wouldn't. You're always going into my room and taking my things. Why can't you leave them alone? Give it back NOW!!'

'You're such a mean old cow. I didn't really want to borrow your stupid necklace anyway!'

My mother was one of five sisters. They didn't have much money or many nice clothes and the motto of the house was 'First up, best dressed'. First up was also first out of the house, to avoid the fury that erupted when her sisters found their favourite clothes had been 'borrowed'.

'Hands Off!'

Taking without asking is almost bound to lead to trouble. If the borrowed item is lost or damaged or simply not returned, the owner is right to be annoyed and the culprit has to make good the loss or damage. It's worth making hard-and-fast rules about 'borrowing' and insisting nobody takes anything without asking first. It is also a good idea to enforce a system for recompensing the owner if anything borrowed is lost or damaged, as this acts as a deterrent to borrowing in the future.

Out of Reach of Temptation

There's an old Danish saying: 'The dog's kennel is not the best place to keep a sausage.' If precious possessions are left within reach of little hands, they're going to be 'borrowed'.

Top Tip: *If younger children are getting into the possessions of the older one, then give the older child a kid-proof place to store them, like a high shelf or a locked cupboard.*

If one of your children repeatedly borrows certain things for everyday use, like scissors or glue, then perhaps it's time for everyone to have their own supply.

6 Violations of Privacy and Space

How to Spot It

This type of squabble is usually simple to spot and the cry of 'Get out of my room!' often precedes it. As your children grow older, they will want more privacy. Younger children may be slow to realise this and trespass into their 'space'.

Border Disputes: Good Fences Make Good Neighbours

Territorial disputes can cause as much trouble in the family home as they can between nations! I know a family where two sons share a bedroom. Down the centre of the room is a piece of tape pinned to the floor. This border is as jealously guarded as any disputed border in the world. This is rather a dramatic solution but clear boundaries make it easier to respect the space and the privacy of others, including siblings.

Agree that private space should be respected. Show respect for your children's space yourself by knocking before going into their rooms, and teach your children to do likewise. Teenage children, in particular, prize their space and privacy, where younger children often have little concept of privacy. Teenagers are entitled to know their possessions won't be disturbed and that, within reason, no one will enter their space without permission.

Will It Stop When They Get Older?

Maybe. But maybe not. Multi-millionaire rock stars Noel and Liam Gallagher, the brothers behind the chart-topping band Oasis, are notorious for their public battles. Big brother Noel pulled out of the band's international tour because he couldn't stand being in the same room as his little brother!

But What Can You Do?

At the end of the day, try to accept that some squabbling is inevitable and, in fact, healthy. You'll never put a stop to it completely. But the next chapter has lots of tips and tricks for making sure things don't get out of hand.

No doubt there are an infinite number of other examples you could add from your own experience. Also, there are deeper, more chronic reasons for siblings to fight – envy, jealousy, rivalry, competitiveness and favouritism. But these are complicated issues, and we'll go into them later in the book (see Chapters 6 and 7).

Stopping the Squabbling

Home Sweet Home?

It's Saturday morning. My friend's two boys have been up for just over an hour. The younger one took his teddy bear to bed with him and woke up in a panic to find his older brother had taken it and hidden it. There was loud shouting while the eight-year-old chased his ten-year-old brother between bedrooms.

A short period of quiet, and then half an hour later each was proclaiming loudly that the other smells.

At breakfast, there was a row about who finished the favourite Crunchy Nut Cornflakes ('It wasn't me!!') and left the other the boring breakfast cereal.

And it's still only nine o'clock.

Certain kinds of low-level warfare, like arguing about stupid things and pestering one another, pass for normal interaction between siblings and seldom cause harm. It may annoy you,

you may wish it wasn't happening, but it really doesn't mean very much.

But there are several things you, as a parent, can do to keep things in check.

Anti-Squabbling Tactics

It's a dirty job but someone's got to do it, and there *are* a few tricks every parent should have up their sleeve:

- the pre-emptive strike
- the policy of non-intervention
- impartial justice
- defensive measures
- negotiate a peace treaty
- accentuate the positive

and (most important) . . .

- know when things are getting out of hand.

1 The Pre-Emptive Strike

Stop It Before It Starts
Do some troubleshooting. Do certain flashpoints cause most of the problems in your family? Do your kids always argue over Saturday morning TV? Are they always convinced the other has more chips? Is there always a dispute about who sits

in the front of the car (best place!) or whose turn it is to sit in the middle (worst place)?

> **Top Tip:** Reduce the likelihood of squabbles by dealing with the things that cause the most persistent fights.

The best solutions to these petty problems are the ones they figure out for themselves.

If it's about possessions, get them to establish rules about sharing. If it's about space, let them divide their shared space in an agreed way. If it's who gets the biggest slice of the pie, use the old trick of asking one to cut and the other to choose, and see what a very refined sense of portion control your kids will develop! If it's about who has the most chips, forget it. There are just some things that aren't worth expending energy on. 'He's got more chips? Well, too bad!'

Peace won't necessarily reign for ever and ever once they have sorted it, but you may get a few days' relief. And when the shouting starts again you can always refer them back to the agreement they made.

> **Top Tip:** Rules may change as your kids get older, but don't allow anarchy around issues that cause rows.

When my husband took our three children to school there were always rows about who sat in the front seat, and at his insistence they decided to take turns. Once a rota was established, there was comparative calm for a few weeks, until one was off school for a few days and the other two went on with the rota. When she started again, there was a row about where they were in the rota, and on that day first in the car got the best seat. The next day, my husband started the rota again and the reason for fighting was removed.

2 The Policy of Non-Intervention

'If You're Going to Squabble, Go Outside'

My uncle and aunt argued all the time, about silly little things. It was a family joke. Once my father commented to my uncle about their bickering and was met with a totally blank expression. 'What do mean, we're always bickering?' said my uncle. 'We don't argue at all!' So, different strokes for different folks. What seemed to be a quarrel to my father was perceived quite differently by my uncle. The same seems to apply to sibling bickering. It often bothers the listener more than those involved; they often seem to do it without thinking.

If you can, ignore bickering and squabbling over things like whose arms are longer, who can eat most spaghetti, which television programme is rubbish . . . and so on. If, however, when faced with this kind of sniping you feel yourself buckling, send them outside, upstairs, to their rooms, turn up the radio or go outside yourself – whatever works for you. As long as you're sure that no one will get hurt, it can alleviate the pressure, at least in the short term.

Stand Back! Interfering Makes It Worse

It's difficult not to rush in and separate them, but if there's no danger to life or limb try to keep out of it. Parental interference ups the ante immediately – all that attention! Watch how much effort goes into trying to prove to a parent that all the blame lies with the other person! If you leave them to their own devices the row will probably peter out, so give it a chance to come to a natural end.

'You're On a Yellow Card!'

If you simply can't bear the noise, and if it looks as though bickering will become something more serious, give your kids a warning. If they don't play together peacefully – or at least quietly – you'll stop the game. A graphic way to issue a warning is the football metaphor 'You're on a yellow card!' This works particularly well with boys. Fear of the subsequent 'red card' and 'sending off' may be just enough to stop them bickering.

3 Impartial Justice

Don't Take Sides

If you are going to get involved in the fights between your children, be very careful how you do it. Don't get drawn into any conversation that begins 'He started it!' or 'It's not fair!' If you didn't see who started it, don't get involved.

> **Top Tip:** Don't intervene by blaming one rather than the other. Remember, THEY are squabbling.

Count to ten and remember the old Dutch saying, 'When two quarrel, both are to blame.' The best answer may even be to say 'Whoever started it, I'm stopping it – now. Go to your rooms!'

Don't Jump to Conclusions

The one who cries loudest is not necessarily the most innocent. Likewise, don't always assume the smaller and weaker child is always the victim. A younger sibling may not be able to overcome a bigger brother or sister in a fight, but a good strategy is to get them into trouble by wailing and crying – and then with a bit of luck maybe they will get a smack from an indignant parent!

A friend recently confessed to getting her big brother into trouble when they were children by deliberately biting her own arm, then running to her mum with the 'evidence'. Her poor brother always got punished, to my friend's evil glee.

Top Tip: *Don't always blame your older child when they fight: the younger child just has less obvious weapons than his fists.*

That Reminds Me . . .

My friend's daughter was claiming loudly that she always got blamed when she had a disagreement with her younger sister. That's a common enough complaint, but in this particular case it took the insight of another member of the family to reveal what was really going on.

He pointed out to my friend that when she was a child the situation was reversed. 'Your mother always took your older sister's side, and maybe you're reacting against that now by always taking your younger daughter's side.'

The past is always with us. What we do now is influenced by our experiences in the past, so as a parent be conscious of your own relationship with your siblings! If you were tormented by your older brother, beware of identifying too much with your younger child and always taking his side. In the same way, if you were always being pestered by your annoying little sister, don't assume a fight is always the fault of your youngest!

4 Defensive Measures

If in Peril – Stop Now!

One of the effects of living with someone for years is that you really know how to wind them up. Wind them up enough and, sure enough, something snaps. Niggling, teasing and sniping gives way to punching, scratching and fighting.

Imagine the scene acted out between a ten-year-old boy and his fourteen-year-old sister. Older sister to younger brother: 'It's horrible the way you eat! It's putting me off my food.' He thumps her. Younger brother to older sister: 'You've got a great big spot on your chin and a huge one on your forehead too. Ugh!! Gross! Pizza face!!' This time *she* punches *him*!

When squabbling gets physical, insist they stop hitting each other immediately. If they don't, pull them apart and, if needs be, send each of them to cool off somewhere. Never smack your children to stop them fighting. A consistent result from psychological research is that physical punishment only encourages aggression in children. You can't teach them not to be aggressive by beating it out of them.

 Top Tip: When fights and name-calling get serious, separate the children until they calm down.

Out of Harm's Way

For children who are used to playing together, when you separate them each is likely to say, 'I don't want to play with him/her anyway!' The reality is often different, and playing alone is hardly ever as much fun as playing with someone else. Give them some time to cool off and take away whatever caused the fight (toy, game, remote control, whatever). An hour alone is often enough for them to have forgotten what the fight was about, and you're quite likely to find them playing peacefully together.

5 Negotiate a Peace Treaty

'Sort It Out Yourselves!'

In Chapter 1, a great deal was made of the fact that siblings can learn from each other how to negotiate and settle differences without having to call in an adult. As a parent, help them do this by wherever possible staying out of their quarrels. At the same time, make them settle their differences. Tell them they have to work out a way of getting on together peacefully if they want to play together, travel in the car together, watch television together, or whatever. In this way you give them an incentive to sort things out between themselves.

 Top Tip: Left to their own devices, even young children can come up with solutions.

When my friend's two daughters came to blows over their 'My Little Pony' game, my friend intervened and told them she would take away all the ponies if they didn't sort out who should have which one. Deep in their game and not wanting to break it up, the girls agreed the little sister could be in charge of the stables and the older girl could have the first choice of pony. Interestingly, this exercise in generosity went beyond the game. Later, preening with virtuous pride, the older daughter came to tell her mother what a kind girl she was; she had let Amy have the best pony *as well as the stables*.

Jaw-Jaw, Not War-War

Winston Churchill said, 'To jaw-jaw is better than to war-war,' and the lesson applies as much to families as to nations. By sorting out differences with their siblings, children can learn there are other ways of solving problems between people than by resorting to fighting. Encourage your children to come up with a solution to the problem that caused the fight. Then leave them to it. Don't solve the problem yourself, and don't act as referee. Tell them to come to you only when they have agreed a solution.

If they complain that they can't agree anything, then suggest a few possibilities like taking turns, tossing a coin or trading favours – for example, big brother can use the computer all afternoon if he fixes little brother's bike first. But don't impose the solution. Let them decide what to do, then let them do it. If they can't or won't, then they have to play alone.

The Silver Lining

When faced with squabbling and fighting, it may seem there is
no upside to sibling conflicts. But there is. Conflict and disagreements are facts of life. When peace finally breaks out between
brothers and sisters, it's because they have used problem-solving
and negotiation skills instead of fighting. These will be very
useful when they have to deal with other children at school and
in the peer group. Indeed, research shows children with siblings
find it easier to settle and make friends when they start school.

6 Accentuate the Positive

Paying Attention to the Right Stuff

Fighting, squabbling and complaining 'It's not fair!' gets a lot
of parental attention. Playing together quietly and co-operating
tends to pass without comment, as relieved parents are just
thankful for a bit of peace and quiet. Unfortunately, this means
that where disruptive behaviour gets attention, good behaviour
doesn't. Show your appreciation! When your children do play
nicely together, make sure you take notice and say something
positive about it.

Try Turning It Around

Next time you catch your kids co-operating with each other,
try saying something along the lines of: 'I really enjoyed playing
Monopoly with you two last night. When both of you join in
together without squabbling, it's really fun.'

Or: 'I know it was boring for you to keep quiet last night

while your brother was revising for his exam, but it was very thoughtful of you. He's lucky to have such a considerate sister.'

 Top Tip: Don't complain that they fight all the time, at least not in front of your children. They'll come to believe it's true and live up to the label!

Boost your children on each other's behalf a little, too – especially with smaller kids: 'Your brother's really happy you don't fiddle with his models any more. He thinks it's very grown up of you.'

Praising them like this might sound a bit forced and unnatural at first but it usually works like a charm. Don't overdo it. Just describe what you see and tell them why you're so pleased about it!

 Top Tip: Help your children to 'make up' and apologise. Teach them not to hold grudges.

7 Know When Things are Getting Out of Hand

Sometimes You *Have* to Get Involved

It would be unrealistic to think all arguments between siblings are just mindless bickering and squabbling and the result of spending too much time together. Sometimes it's serious, and then it's time for parents to intervene. Parents often ask when they should get involved, but generally the answer is to do it when the situation becomes so severe that you have no alternative *but* to do something. If any of the following apply, then it is time to take action:

- if the dispute disrupts the whole household;
- if it goes on and on and there seems to be no sign of reconciliation;
- if the children can't make progress by themselves;
- if one child is suffering;
- if there is regular bullying or hurtful teasing.

75

Top Tip: *If you believe there is an underlying issue of jealousy or some other frustration, then more discussion with the child is necessary.*

Sticks and Stones . . .

Not all fighting is physical. There's also name-calling, teasing and other types of verbal bullying. Some teasing is normal, but it should be kept firmly in check.

Sticks and stones may break my bones but words will never hurt me? In reality, words often hurt more than any blow. Constant teasing throughout childhood can cause a lifelong sense of inferiority and low self-esteem. This is an account of one woman's experiences at the hands of her older sister:

> I was never very good at school. Looking back I think I was dyslexic but no one knew about such things in those days. My older sister teased me mercilessly about my writing and my poor reading. I would never pick up a book at home, because as soon as she saw me she would start on me and I would end up in tears. It was hard enough for me at school and she just added to it at home. The whole thing just ruined my chances of getting anything out of my education.
>
> (courtesy: raisingkids.co.uk)

Watch What You Say

Sometimes name-calling is just thoughtless: 'You smell! Naa-naaa!' 'Who cut your hair? The council?' and sometimes teasing is an exercise in power or anger: 'I can stay up till eight o'clock. You're not allowed! You're a baby!' or 'I don't care if you borrowed my make-up, you've still got a face like an elephant's bottom.'

Other comments may be more hurtful and have longer effects. I know a woman whose sister told her throughout her childhood, 'Nobody loves you.' She came from a family where people didn't talk about their feelings and was therefore never reassured that she was loved. To this day she is affected by the cruelty of her sister.

Don't Make Personal Comments

Then there are the things that just don't need to be said. Everyone has something they are sensitive about and siblings have an inbuilt sensor for what offends. I saw a young boy in a restaurant slam his spoon down on his plate so hard that the food splashed all over the table. What caused him to react so violently? His older sister's remarks about his eating habits. 'What did I do?' she protested innocently. 'I just told him not to make so much noise when he chews!'

Easing the Teasing

What should you do if you hear one of your children being cruel and unkind to their sibling? The major thing is to stop serious teasing and personal abuse or someone will be hurt by it. Lay down some house rules. Tell your children that, if they're angry and upset with their brother or sister, there are other ways to express it than by personal abuse. Instead of name-calling, ask them to try stating what it is that's made them feel upset or angry. Use 'I' language, such as 'I'm very angry when you use my things without asking,' or 'I don't like it when you make personal comments about me in front of my friends.'

If it's thoughtless cruelty or unkindness, point out to the perpetrator that words can wound. Give them an example of something that maybe they said as a joke, or 'didn't mean anything' by, but which nevertheless was very hurtful. 'I know you were only joking, but Nadeem really took it to heart when you said she was fat.' Remind them perhaps of the times they have been wounded by the thoughtless or malicious comments of a friend or member of the family.

What If It Persists?

There may be a physical reason for the teasing. Perhaps one of your children is overweight or suffering from acne, or has wonky teeth. Your doctor or dentist will be able to help with the physical – but it's important to counteract the teasing as well. Otherwise, the tormentor usually just finds another reason to needle his or her sibling.

Deal with it from both sides. Encourage the victim to walk away if possible, or simply ignore it. It's not much fun needling someone if they refuse to rise to the bait. My youngest daughter was quite touchy and often reacted to teasing – not always unkind – by storming off. Once after an episode like this, I pointed out to her that when she reacts so strongly the other person feels they have 'won'. I encouraged her to try to ignore it in future, and it worked.

> **Top Tip:** *If they're really having problems, teach them a few good put-downs. With the right delivery, 'So?' or 'Yeah – right...' or a serious 'Do you really think so?' can stop the teaser in his or her tracks.*

Another strategy is to react to teasing by going 'over the top'. Here's an example my neighbour's son used when his younger brother made a snide remark about his spots.

Younger brother: 'You've got spots, naa-naaa!'
Older brother: 'You're right. I have got spots. I've got millions of spots. Tons of them. I probably have more spots than anyone else in the world. You're so-o-o observant!'

Not a lot you could say to that, is there?

What about the perpetrator? If the teasing goes on then you may have to introduce penalties to stop it. Discourage the teaser with pocket-money fines or loss of privileges.

And Finally . . .

Look at your family as a whole, too. Are there any adults who are role-modelling this type of teasing with their own behaviour? Are you? If so, try and avoid it in front of your children.

Deeper Feelings

Superficial squabbles flare up quickly and die down just as fast. Deeper feelings can smoulder for much longer. One or more of your children may be jealous, envious or resentful of their brother or sister, and problems can be accelerated by too much competition between siblings or feelings of favouritism. The next two chapters explain how these long-standing problems start and what you, as a parent, can do about them.

Sibling Rivalry

As brothers and sister jostle for position and before they work out ways of living together, there are the wars that precede the settlements. These are arguments about sharing, about fairness, about privacy, about possessions and about absolutely nothing at all. There are scraps and hitting, pushing and pulling and just getting in the way.

And as if that wasn't enough, there's teasing, name-calling and shouting. From the older ones there is bossing and occasionally bullying. From the younger ones there is whining and crying and complaining: 'She hit me!' 'He's calling me names!' 'She's picking on me!' 'He took my toy ... book ... blanket ... clothes ... trainers ...' The list is endless.

What's at the Root of the Problem?

When people talk about 'sibling rivalry', what do they mean, exactly? If your children aren't getting on, it can show itself in many different ways. As they say, all happy families resemble one another, but each unhappy family is unhappy in its own way.

As a parent, you'll know your children well enough to judge when daily squabbles are turning into something more serious.

Is the competition between your kids persistent and determined? Do they dislike spending time together? Perhaps play fights are becoming more violent. Maybe you can see an intention to cause bodily harm, or perhaps someone is being truly malicious. When everyday teasing becomes spiteful, or when one child is being bullied by the other, things are getting out of hand. You have a case of sibling rivalry.

Quiet Doesn't Always Mean Peace

The family is a very small group and if two or three of its members can't get along together then everyone will be affected. One father, despairing of the relationships between his two sons, aged fourteen and twelve, wrote: 'this situation has been on-going for the last couple of years and is now becoming intolerable'.

Your children may not make a big outward show of their feelings. Instead, your boisterous toddler may become subdued and withdrawn. Teenagers spend more time with their friends than their family – it's a normal part of growing up – but it's not normal for them to constantly ignore or avoid their brother or sister.

 Top Tip: *A good sulk for a few days shouldn't have you rushing to conclusions, but watch out for prolonged periods of discord.*

Rivalry, Jealousy and Envy

What are the emotions behind serious fallings-out and sustained sibling rivalry? All families are different but, very broadly speaking, the usual culprits are feelings of jealousy; a persistent sense of unfairness; competitiveness and one-upmanship; and, unfortunately, plain dislike. At the heart of all these emotions is comparing, which makes siblings ask questions like:

- Do they love him more than they love me?
- Why does she get more attention?
- Do they think she is cleverer, funnier, nicer, more lovable than me?
- Does he get more of things than I do?

1 Jealousy

Everybody gets jealous sometimes. As adults, you and your partner will realise that 'love is not a pie' – meaning there's an inexhaustible supply of affection for everyone. You can dish out love to all your family members without ever running out of it! Sometimes, however, your children need help to understand this.

Move Over!

The firstborn is particularly hit by the introduction of another child into the family. The firstborn has the full-time attention of two doting adults and quite possibly four adoring grandparents, and then suddenly the spotlight shifts and another child is commanding all the attention. However careful the parents are to minimise the effects, there is no denying the fact that only half the parental attention is now available. No wonder the displaced child feels jealous towards the newcomer.

That feeling of having to make space for the newcomer and the feelings of jealousy that come along with it have a lasting effect. Psychologists report the firstborn is more prone to feelings of jealousy than later-born children. On the topic of sibling rivalry, one mum wrote:

> Going back to when they were young, the eldest child would bite and pinch the second child, till we had to shut the second child in the bedroom, out of harm's way.
>
> (courtesy: raisingkids.co.uk)

Sibling Fact

Believe it or not, research has shown babies as young as four months old are capable of experiencing and showing jealousy!

Sibling rivalry is a reality. It may come and go as the children grow, and many siblings who were deadly rivals throughout their childhood become close confidants and good friends as adults. But sometimes the jealousies can last throughout siblings' lives.

Award-winning novelists Antonia Byatt and Margaret Drabble played out their jealousies in the public eye when Byatt won the Booker Prize, to her hitherto better-known sister's pique. Antonia Byatt's book *The Game* is about two sisters, both writers, and their mutually destructive relationship.

> **Top Tip:** Hope for the best. Expect sibling relationships to change over the years – sometimes they'll be good friends and sometimes not.

In some cases, jealousy becomes so severe that it affects the whole household. In one instance, two teenage brothers fell out over a girl they both liked, and refused to make eye contact for over two years. The situation only improved when the eldest went off to college and they both had a little breathing space to cool down.

A friend of mine admitted being so jealous of her 'cuter' younger sister that she didn't want her to make friends when she started secondary school.

We didn't look alike. I'm fairly dark and was going through a grungy phase whereas she looked like Alice in Wonderland and was always a very sweet, tidy little girl. I was a few years older, and I suppose a spotty, bad-tempered adolescent wasn't as appealing as she was! I was sick of her getting all the attention. I started a nasty rumour by telling everybody she'd been adopted and her real father was some sort of criminal or murderer or something. Looking back on it, it was a truly horrible thing to do to her.

What to Do
The root of feelings of jealousy is when one child feels the other gets special treatment or more attention or is loved more than they are. The way to deal with this feeling is obvious: be fair in your dealings with your children and make sure they know you value them equally for who they are. There is more information on how feelings of jealousy and rivalry are activated and how to deal with them in the next chapter.

2 'It's Not Fair'

If I had a pound for every time I heard 'It's not fair!' I'd have become a millionaire before my kids graduated from nursery school.

A few examples illustrate the point:

'It's not fair, she doesn't have to wash up.'
'It's not fair, he's got more sausages than me!'
'It's not fair, why should I have to go to bed before him?'
'It's not fair, she gets more pocket money than me.'
'It's not fair, you helped him with his homework and you won't help me.'

Within the family, brothers and sisters pay very close attention to who gets what, and more often than not feel they don't get enough. A very refined sense of what is fair usually means 'I want more than I'm getting'! I have yet to hear a child complain 'It's not fair!' because they think they are getting more than they deserve.

One dad complained: 'My kids are always saying, "It's not fair." I do everything I can to make things fair but it's never fair enough.'

Spell It Out

Where there are differences in how much each child gets, then they have to be explained. You may think it's obvious that one should get more because they're older, younger, in need of more help, not so good at maths or whatever, but your other child – or children – may not be able to work it out for themselves. Once you have spelled out why there are differences, be consistent and don't give way just because one moans, 'It's not fair.' Change when the situation changes, but don't give in to blackmail when one claims unfair treatment.

Some parents are very susceptible to complaints about fairness and will go to ridiculous lengths to make everything exactly the same. One mother I know buys presents for all of her children whenever one of them has a birthday, 'so the others won't feel left out'. In my opinion not only does this show excessive concern that all should be treated equally, but it also detracts from the specialness of the birthday.

Other parents take a more robust approach. Refusing to measure and apportion everything so it is exactly equivalent, they tell their kids they've done what they think is best, and if it's not precisely fair... well, nor is life. Too much emphasis on making everything the same only leads to increasing concern about who gets what. I asked one dad I know, with four noisy kids under twelve, how he copes with day-in, day-out complaints of 'It's not fair!'

I don't do fair. I tell my kids it's not fair when parents put their cigarettes out on their children, or when whole families have to survive on a bowl of rice a day. When four well-fed, well-looked-after kids start fighting over who gets the last chocolate, it's not worth worrying about.

 Top Tip: Don't get drawn into arguments about what's 'fair'.

---

3 One-Upmanship and Competitiveness

One of Harry Enfield's most unappealing characters is the dad who is so competitive that he always has to win – even when playing games with his kid and his wife, he simply *has* to beat them. The spectacle of a grown man running rings around two little kids in his desperate rush to score a goal, or his triumph in bowling his wife out at cricket, is laughable, unless it's *your* father. These are families where it's not playing the game but winning that counts.

I know a father like this. He has three sons, and everything they do is measured against how other children do. Once Son

Number Two got 95 per cent in a maths exam. 'Was that the highest score?' his father asked him. When he was told the highest score was 96 per cent, his father said, 'Next time you get 97 per cent.' The boys – not surprisingly – are very competitive with each other. Interestingly, though all three are sporty, they have each opted for very different sports – less surprisingly none of them a team sport!

Sometimes the competition is limited and doesn't extend through all areas of life. When tennis aces Venus and Serena Williams played against each other at Wimbledon, their father refused to watch their match, saying he couldn't cheer for either against the other. Though competing on court, off court they relate well and support each other. The Schumacher brothers compete against each other on the motor-racing circuit, both vying to be the World Formula One champion.

Star-Crossed Siblings

But for some siblings competition never ends. Hollywood starlets Olivia de Havilland and Joan Fontaine didn't speak to each other for the whole of the 1940s! Joan was nominated for the same Oscar as her sister Olivia, and Olivia was hotly tipped to win. When – to everybody's surprise – Joan Fontaine won instead, her first reaction was fear of how her older sister would react to being pipped to the post.

There may be less at stake in your own back garden, but the rivalry may be just as fierce.

'I'm Better Than You Are!'

Day to day you can see it all the time, an on-going lesson in one-upmanship between brothers and sisters, each competing to be better than the other. The younger one fighting for supremacy, the older one intent on maintaining position as top dog.

Listen to the following exchanges between two brothers overheard in just a single evening!

On the way home from school: 'Let's race!' says the younger one, knowing he'll beat his older brother, who is less athletic. They race, the younger one wins, and how he gloats! 'You're such a slow coach!'

At home: They're playing computer games. This time, the older one is streets ahead in the game. 'You're pathetic at this,' he says. 'Well, it's a stupid game anyway,' says the younger. 'Naah, you're just saying that because you're no good at it!' says his brother.

Tea time: 'I can eat my spaghetti faster than you!' (Mum puts a stop to that one).

Homework time: The younger one asks for help with his maths. 'I could easily do that when I was in your class,' says the older one.

Bed time: The younger one asks his mother how to pronounce a certain word in a book he is reading. 'Magid doesn't know how to read!!! Yah yah yah . . .'

91

What If It's True?

What parents do (or don't do) is only part of the sibling story. There's also the rivalry that arises, from having a sibling who *is* always that much bigger, cleverer, more athletic or funnier than you are.

When a big sister has her nose put out of joint by a know-it-all little brother, or little brother is dominated and subdued by an overbearing big sister, then trouble is looming. Do any of these situations seem familiar?

I think Stephen is jealous of Laura's natural ability at things, whereas he has to work hard at them. It's very hard for him when he sees how easily it comes to her.

My eldest daughter is academically very bright and our youngest isn't. I feel this is difficult for her to follow. We try to overcome it as much as possible but I feel she still lives in the shadow.

Sara's not so bright and Michael is fifteen months younger and breathing down her neck . . . he comes on superior to her, and no matter what you do or say, it must grate. How would you feel having a brother who says, 'I know!' before you've even looked up the answer?

These differences are real. Many of them have to do with academic achievement or simply being quicker and cleverer. Parents naturally take a lot of pride in the achievements of their children, and a less academically able sibling may feel inadequate in the eyes of his parents.

However, recognising each child as being not 'best' but with their own unique, special abilities can help both siblings feel they're equally loved and valued. A friend's eldest daughter was an academic star from an early age but her younger sister – although bright – just wasn't in the same league at school. As their mum explains:

> Lauren was always top of the class but Caroline has always been fantastic at anything practical. Even when they were both small, Caroline would make elaborate tents in the garden and create wonderful 'camp food' – Lauren preferred to sit inside the tent and read. Caroline decided not to follow her sister to university but went to catering college instead. I've always been proud of my girls, but now that one has an MSc and the other works in an award-winning restaurant, I can hardly get my head through the door when I'm out with them!

4 Just the Wrong Chemistry

> 'I hate you!'
> 'I hate you, too!'

Brothers and sisters may say this, but do they ever mean it? When I was researching sibling rivalry, one mum told me the following story:

> When my younger son was born, our eldest boy became very jealous. He was so violent towards the baby that we never

dared leave them together unsupervised. Later, when they went to the same school, the older boy ignored his younger brother totally. They never spoke to each other at school and passed each other coming home from school each evening without saying anything.

Sometimes it's not outright hatred but just indifference, as this person posted on the raisingkids.co.uk discussion board:

I never particularly got on with my brother and don't have many happy memories of us growing up together. I always seemed to have more fun with my friends. After I left home, we just drifted apart. Neither of us makes a particular effort to see each other and we meet up once every couple of years or so. I think my parents would like us to be closer but it's not going to happen, I'm afraid. I don't bear him any particular ill-will but we're just not very well suited as people.

What Can You Do About These Feelings?

Sometimes negative emotions can be simply a result of circumstances or different abilities – it would take a saint not to be slightly jealous of a better-looking big brother who sat his GCSEs a year early to concentrate on playing football for the Scotland Under-18 squad! Sometimes parents foster bad feeling – often with the best intentions or just without realising it – with favouritism, labelling, comparing or preferential treatment. The next chapter will show you how to bring out the best in your children's relationships with each other.

Comparing, Labelling and Favouritism

The Roots of Rivalry

Comparing is at the root of sibling rivalry. When a child believes that a brother or sister is more accomplished or better able to please their parents, they start to compete for parental attention and praise and they grow to resent their sibling. No child wants to feel in an way 'less' in the eyes of his parents.

Yet sometimes only one person in the family has a special claim to fame, and often it's encouraged by the parents' own values, hopes and dreams.

For example, Nuala has an exceptionally clever firstborn, Stuart, who's recently won a scholarship to one of the leading schools in the area. It's hard for her to avoid boasting about his achievements – well, she's very proud of him – but it makes it

difficult for Sarah, her younger one (who's not at all academically gifted) to find her place in the sun.

Sometimes children like Sarah look for a different way to excel – maybe music, sports or art. But if they have no natural talent in these areas, they may decide to be best at being naughty – and 'naughty' usually gets a lot of attention!

Top Tip: *Recognise each child is an individual and unique.*

Does Birth Order Matter?

Maybe there's no particular 'star of the show' in your family. Does this mean you'll have no problems with rivalry? Probably not!

Children from the same family and home environment often show remarkable differences in personality and behaviour. Why should that be?

Although some differences can be put down to inherited temperament, there is also an effect caused by the child's position in the family. While many factors affect the development of children, parents can understand their children better if they know how they are affected by their position in the family.

Firstborn: Oldest, First and Best?

'I was here first!'

Firstborns often try and find their place within the family by being responsible, helpful . . . and sometimes a little too perfectionist! Used to being at the centre of attention, when Baby Number Two arrives they get to be the boss.

Over-Achieving and Over-Anxious

Proud parents have very high expectations of their firstborn. They lavish a lot of attention and encouragement on their child but at the same time (as novice parents themselves) they are anxious and concerned. As a result, the over-achievement of the firstborn is well documented; they try hard to please and it shows in their success at school and work.

At the same time, they are more anxious than their younger siblings, who have had the advantage of being brought up by parents who have grown more confident. Spending more time with adults, the firstborn tends to be more conforming and respectful of authority when compared to later-born children. Being Number One in the family, a firstborn tends to be bossy. Firstborn girls are often more 'motherly' and supportive to younger children in the family.

> **Top Tip:** *Firstborns often feel the need to be responsible, so give them lots of opportunity to be silly, and generally 'loosen up' – let them learn that it's okay to fail and that they don't need to aim for 100 per cent perfection.*

Born to be Wild?

When Child Number Two (or Three) comes along, Mum and Dad are more relaxed in their parenting. As a result, the children are inclined to be more 'chilled out'. A second-born child finds the role of 'helpful and responsible' is already taken. It's difficult to be the best at school when your sibling has the advantage of age and experience, so many second-borns major in sociability, becoming easygoing, co-operative and generally more popular.

SHE'S OUR SECOND CHILD – DRIVES US MAD EVERY SECOND. –

Where firstborns fill a family niche all by themselves and develop a 'mind set' that looks to their parents, later-born children are more intent on making themselves different from their siblings and having their own space. Younger siblings in particular are very sensitive to comparisons with their older siblings and deal with this by becoming quite different from Child Number One.

Top Tip: *Don't overload the eldest and don't let them lord it over their siblings. Don't use them as unpaid babysitters.*

Recent research reveals the firstborn as more concerned with pleasing his parents and later-borns as more concerned with challenging their siblings. Each develops attitudes reflecting this early conditioning. One of the major differences is that firstborns are more likely to be conservative thinkers and upholders of the *status quo*. Later-borns are 'born to rebel'.

Sibling Fact

Almost all of the really radical breakthroughs in philosophy, political theory or science come not from firstborns but from 'later-borns'!

Stuck in the Middle with You

Middle child may feel squeezed and develop a sense that life is not fair, being neither the heir apparent nor little Prince Charming. Middle children are assumed to be good diplomats and perhaps a little bit devious, a result of being neither the 'big one' nor the baby and struggling to find a position. They often act as go-betweens and peacemakers.

Top Tip: *Does the squeaky wheel always get the most oil? Remember to give your middle child lots of contact on a one-to-one basis to prevent them feeling overlooked.*

Last but Not Least

The 'baby' of the family will be spoiled and dependent on their parents, but also a rule-breaker. In my own research, one of the clearest findings was that in a three-child family the youngest was most often the mother's favourite. Youngest child might decide to be cute, entertaining and needing to be taken care of, and so learn the skills of charm and manipulation.

 Top Tip: *Take your youngest child seriously and give him a chance to act 'grown up' and be responsible.*

Take a look at your own family and see if your children fit into 'birth-order roles' – but remember, these are only guides and there are always exceptions to the rule!

Sibling Facts

Apparently, a middle child is less likely to end up in prison or to commit suicide than his or her siblings! Other research has shown that having one elder brother decreases a boy's chances of being thought physically attractive, and having several older brothers increases the effect.

Comparing

If siblings compare themselves with each other it can cause bad feeling. Parents shouldn't add to the problem by making comparisons themselves.

But it's so easy to do, isn't it? One of your children is being a real pain in the neck and the other is as good as gold. How easy it is to turn to the 'naughty' one and contrast his behaviour with your good child. Your little girl hangs on to her mother's skirt and won't say hello to your visitors. To try and encourage her, you point out how nicely her brother said hello. Why do we do it? To show that it can be done? To motivate the reluctant, naughty child to behave like the sociable, good one?

 Top Tip: Don't compare your children – 'Comparing is a death knell to sibling harmony' (Elizabeth Fishel, 1980).

Comparing makes your children into competitors rather than allies. Telling one he's much better at making friends than his sister or telling the other she's much better behaved than her brother builds up barriers between them. If you're constantly drawing comparisons, your kids will think everything is a competition – even who gets to the bathroom first.

Comparisons Don't Motivate

My daughter is easy-going and helpful, unlike my son who's so naughty he's driving me mad! What can I do?

My eldest is fantastic at school but why isn't his little brother as clever?

My little girl has lovely manners but her brother's an embarrassment!

How would you feel at work if your boss showed you a colleague's presentation and then asked why you couldn't manage to produce a professional piece of work like her? Would you say, 'Yes, good point, I'll try harder next assignment'? Probably not! You might even start thinking of a career change.

It's the same with siblings. If you make one child feel 'bad' it's likely they'll become worse, not better. As one boy said, 'If I can't be good, I'll be the best at being bad.'

Remember your schooldays? Unfortunately, once they'd become recognised as the class troublemaker, most 'bad boys' (or girls) felt they had to live up to their dubious reputations.

 Top Tip: *Remember, your children should feel they are valued for themselves, as unique individuals who each have their own special qualities and talents.*

Don't Compare Directly . . .

If one of your children isn't as successful or well behaved as his or her sibling, the first thing to do is take a look at their behaviour on its own, without any reference to their brothers or sisters. A comparison is always a put-down for one child and is likely to drive a wedge between your kids.

. . . But Don't Compare Indirectly, Either

Comparisons that make one child shine should be avoided, too, since these are usually an implied criticism of the other. Saying, 'You get on with your homework as soon as you come home . . .' implies '. . . unlike your sister, who has to be forced to do her assignments.' Telling one child 'You're always so neat and tidy . . .' carries the implication '. . . which is so much better than your scruffy brother.'

Top Tip: *Don't try and make one child look good by doing the other one down.*

Highlighting the shortcomings of a sibling won't make them friends. Avoid saying things like 'You're always so cheerful – much better than your baby brother, who's always crying.' It encourages rivalry and undermines the relationship between your children. Instead, try and work with your children to build positive and supportive relationships between them.

How to Encourage Better Behaviour without Comparing

How can you help one child be 'less naughty'? Decide what behaviour you want to see less of and try to ignore it whenever possible. It may seem strange that complaints, being shouted at or even a smack could be something your child wants, but sometimes any attention is better than no attention. If it has to be negative attention, at least it's attention. If attention is the oxygen of bad behaviour then ignore bad behaviour.

Top Tip: *If you give attention to the 'naughty' behaviour it only encourages more!*

Attention = Reward!

Concentrate on changing your child's view of him or herself so they don't think of themselves as a 'naughty girl' or 'bad boy'. Focus on the good behaviour when it happens. Tell them what you notice, when you notice it. Say what you feel about certain types of behaviour and what it is you expect. Below are some rules for encouraging good behaviour without referring to anyone else's behaviour.

- **Describe what you see without comparing.**
  Instead of saying:
  'Even the baby has better table manners than you,'
  say:
  'The sauce is dripping off your spoon on to the tablecloth.'

- **Describe what you see by referring to his or her behaviour only.**
  Instead of saying:
  'You've got such nice manners, unlike some people I could mention,'
  say:
  'Grandma was very pleased when you thanked her so nicely for lunch.'

- **Describe what you expect.**
  Instead of saying:
  'Your brother doesn't need to be told twenty times to wash up,'
  say:
  'I expect you to do the washing up straight away after dinner.'

Labelling

The ancient Romans had a tradition of naming twin babies as 'opposites'. They believed twins were one person split into two, so one would be the reverse of the other. If a pair of twins were named 'Loquax' and 'Antiloquax', the Romans assumed one would be a chatterbox and the other one would scarcely talk at all. This often turned out to be a self-fulfilling prophecy, as few people would feel inclined to start up a conversation with a child called 'Untalkative'.

Although this custom died out a long time ago, many families still decide one of their children is 'the sporty one' and the other is 'the clever one'. One family insisted their son was 'the maths person' while their daughter was 'artistic' – even when she scored higher than her brother in Maths A level! Sometimes labelling can be more harmful, when one child is tagged 'the black sheep of the family'.

'Give a Dog a Bad Name . . .'

'Keep on telling me that's what I am, and that's what I'll become . . .' so be careful how you describe your children.

It's human nature to put things – and people – into categories. The English language is full of 'wicked witches', 'mad scientists' and 'nutty professors'. But these labels are seldom the whole truth – or true at all. If a curvaceous model prangs her car, she's a 'typical woman driver'; if we are told that she's a blonde . . . well, enough said! If a forty-year-old businessman had a similar mishap, most people would think it was simple bad luck.

A friend recently locked her keys into her flat before flying off to a conference in Geneva. Describing the incident, she laughingly told me she was just being a typical absent-minded academic. This woman has a PhD in Applied Physics and builds bespoke computers in her spare time for fun, besides being one of the most organised people I've ever come across!

Labelling is Lazy

Sometimes a label can be a bit of a joke. In other circumstances it can offend people. With children who lack the life-experience to take labels with a pinch of salt, they can believe every word you say and act accordingly. After all, your kids trust you to tell them the truth.

Listen to what family members say about each other. Consider the nicknames, the stories told about each other and the jokes. These are signs the family members are cast into roles and given labels to match:

'Oh, he's the clever one in the family but he's got no common sense.'

'She's a bit of a tearaway.'

'My youngest is such a scaredy cat, she's nervous about absolutely everything!'

Labelling is Disabling

It may be true your clever son has his head in the clouds, or your daughter is a bit of a wild-child, or your youngest is particularly cautious. However, labelling them as 'scatty', 'rebellious' or 'fearful' will only make things worse.

 Top Tip: *Labels – good and bad ones – become part of your child's self-image.*

A label may start with only a germ of truth in it but it quickly acquires its own force. A 'clumsy' child becomes apprehensive about picking up something delicate and drops it in a state of nervousness. More proof that he is clumsy!

Good Labels and Bad Labels: Labels in Pairs

Parents often label their children by comparing and contrasting them. Firstborns are often 'nervous and shy' while their younger siblings are 'outgoing and sociable'.

111

Children of different genders are sometimes offset against each other: 'Mummy's little soldier' and 'Daddy's little princess'. Some labels link a child to other members of their family: 'You're just like your father!'

Labelled with Love

Sometimes labels are given affectionately but convey equally powerful messages: 'My little fusspot!' or 'My son, the urban terrorist!'

In one family, the eldest daughter was always expected to take after her father, a lawyer. He was proud of his clever, argumentative daughter and called her 'my little QC'. After a three-year law course, she plucked up the courage to tell him she really wanted to do an English Literature degree. Her father was disappointed but realised she'd be happier doing what she enjoyed rather than what she felt was expected of her.

In another family, the eldest boy was light-heartedly told he was stand-offish. At family gatherings, his parents always said, 'Oh, don't expect a kiss from Brian!' Years later, at his grandfather's funeral, he stood back from comforting his grandmother because he felt it would be 'weird' and out of character, while his more 'affectionate' siblings hugged her.

Even Good Labels Can Be Bad

Positive labels have their downsides as well as negative ones. A child constantly labelled as 'the responsible one' in the family feels he always has to be on best behaviour. If he acts 'irresponsibly', what will people think? His 'real self' can be responsible *and* reckless. Sometimes he feels the desire to break out and be devil-may-care but the label inhibits him. He may also be afraid his parents only like his 'responsible self' and won't like the 'real boy' if they see it.

Mixed Messages

Some labels may mostly be about fulfilling your need as a parent. Ask yourself what your motives are. Sometimes an apparently negative label conveys a mixed message. The parents of an 'urban terrorist' may be secretly proud of his energy and recklessness. A 'fearful' child brings out a strong nurturing instinct, and everybody likes to feel wanted. Do you like having your 'nervous' child turn to you for reassurance? Is your 'tearaway' doing the things you always wanted to do but never dared?

You're the adult, so it's up to you to look at your feelings and work out what's best for your children. Perhaps that means gently weaning a fearful child away from his reliance on you and helping him stand on his own two feet. Maybe you can help your 'wild-child' see that risky behaviour won't always be in her best interests.

Undoing the Labels

If you've got a 'scatterbrain' or a 'loner' on your hands, how can you undo the label? If the labels become part of your child's self-image, you need to change the way they see themselves.

Top Tip: *To change the label, change the message.*

Imagine how you'd like your child to feel about herself. Then send messages that help her see herself differently. A 'lazy' child could become co-operative, helpful and energetic. A 'tearaway' could be steadier and more focused. Once you've got the idea clear in your own head, start sending messages to this effect by your words and your actions.

'You Can Be Different if You Want to Be'

Reinforce good behaviour. Catch them doing something right and show you've noticed. If a 'lazy' child lays the table without being asked, comment approvingly and – most important – leave it at that.

Recognise what's been done by saying something like 'Thanks for setting the table, that's a big help,' but – and this is really critical – don't follow it up by saying something like 'See! You can do it if you want to!' Give the acknowledgement without referring back to their 'usual behaviour'.

 Top Tip: *Resist the temptation to compare 'new, improved' behaviour with the 'usual' behaviour.*

Don't go overboard with the praise. After all, laying the table is only normal, courteous behaviour. If you start saying, 'That's wonderful, you're *so* helpful!' soon your child will expect a standing ovation for washing out the bathtub. 'Drip feed' with a little praise wherever appropriate.

Show a Little Faith
Avoid telling your child how 'lazy' or 'noisy' or 'boisterous' they are. Don't act as if they are, either. If you get irritated because you don't get the help you want in the house, don't do it yourself. Expect good behaviour, and sooner or later good behaviour will follow.

 Top Tip: Say 'when' – not 'if'.

When your child plays up to the label they've been given, say how you feel about it and what kind of behaviour you expect. Be firm and assertive. Don't talk about how irresponsible or short-tempered they are, talk about how you feel and what you feel appropriate behaviour to be. Instead of saying, 'You're such a lazybones!' say, 'I don't like having to ask you to tidy your room over and over again. I expect you to do it when I ask you to.'

Assume your child will do it. Say, 'You can watch TV *when* you've washed up' or '*When* will you be able to help me in the garden this weekend?' If your daughter's not great at getting

115

up in the morning, only call her once. If she ignores it and is late for school, let her take the consequences, but use the opportunity to talk to her about it afterwards.

This course of action is tough. It often seems easier to do it yourself. You'll probably feel guilty if your child is late for school, and dirty dishes piling up in the sink may drive you mad. But there's no gain without pain.

Don't worry – it will eventually pay off, to the benefit of the whole family. Everyone has to learn the lesson that you can't expect to get away with being careless, lazy or always late, and the best place to learn that lesson is at home.

Set a Good Example

Be a good role model but try not to make it obvious you're setting yourself up as an example. Say matter-of-factly, 'I don't feel like clearing up now, but it has to be done so I'd better get on with it,' or 'I've had a rotten day at work and it's a real effort not to snap.' Just say it and do it, without meaningful looks in your child's direction!

It Ain't Necessarily So . . .

A child who is labelled is often reminded how 'true' the label is. Parents can often help undo the label by recalling occasions when the label wasn't correct. If one child says his brother is 'rubbish at getting up in the morning', remind them he got up early on holiday without any problem at all!

Favouritism

Joseph's dad gave him a splendid coat of many colours – the equivalent of a flash pair of top-of-the-range trainers in the days of the pharaohs. His ten older brothers weren't impressed by this blatant display of favouritism and threw Joseph down a well.

Put simply, favouritism means showing a marked preference for one of your children and giving him or her particular love and attention. It's no coincidence that, in horse racing, 'favourite' means 'the one expected to win'.

As children develop their own personalities, a natural warmth may grow between one child and a parent. They may have the same outlook on life, similar interests or a shared sense of humour. This may lead to accusations of favouritism.

You Like Him More Than You Like Me!

Jealousy and envy are facts of life for many families. But where do they come from? Children expect to be loved and treated equally by their parents, and if they see favouritism they resent it bitterly.

 Top Tip: *Parents are human. Sometimes it's easier to get on with one of your children than another – that doesn't make you a bad parent.*

One child may share your interests, have your temperament, or be more fun. Maybe one of your children is vulnerable and you feel particularly protective of him. Another may remind you of a relative you didn't particularly like and it colours your relationship with that child.

Am I Second-Best?

To the child who gets less attention or feels they are 'less fun', this is difficult to accept. They want everything to be shared equally, including their parents' love and attention, and when it's not they cry favouritism. Most parents feel uncomfortable at the idea of having a favourite and try to conceal it from the other children, but not all parents are so fair-minded.

As a child, my friend Gina had a very pretty sister. When they were children, their mother was very proud of her sister's good looks. She constantly admired her and loved to buy her nice clothes. Gina herself is very attractive, but when someone compliments her on her appearance her first thought is 'Yes, but you should see my sister.' Incidentally, her sister's good looks didn't last. Now, as an adult, she suffers from feelings of low self-esteem because so much of her childhood identity was tied up with being 'such a pretty girl!'

'Am I Less Lovable?'

Parents who have favourites and make little or no effort to hide it cause emotional damage to the 'unfavoured child'. All of us feel we should be special to our parents and loved for who we are. When children see signs that they are less well regarded than their siblings, it is hurtful and it makes them angry. They ask themselves, 'Why don't my parents love me as much as they love her? Is it because I am less lovable?'

These effects can last a lifetime. We receive many emails about sibling relationships, including the following, from an adult visitor to our site still struggling to come to terms with favouritism in her childhood and still concerned with the unfair behaviour of her mother.

As the less favoured child, I feel favouritism has had severe repercussions on my character. An example would be the way I am *obsessed* with the avoidance of double standards and with being consistent in the things I say and do. I feel this is unhealthy but the problem that bugs me most is that my mom has recently revealed that, in her opinion, favouritism is *entirely* the fault of the child. And she acts this way.

(courtesy: raisingkids.co.uk)

It's Tough at the Top

It's not only the unfavoured child who can suffer from the effects of favouritism. It may not be so great for the favourite, either. An innate sense of fairness may make the favoured child feel guilty that his sibling is overlooked. They may regret the lack of sibling closeness they see in other families. Parental expectations may be too high and the chosen child may fear they will be a disappointment. If they don't achieve, or are naughty, then they fear a fall from grace and becoming the unfavoured one. And they know how rotten that would be!

119

Recognise the Situation

If one of your children says, 'You love him more than you love me,' your first reaction is most likely to be, 'Of course not, I love all my children equally.' However, many parents do find one child easier to get on with.

Tell-Tale Signs

All children claim, 'It's not fair!' but now-and-then favouritism is likely to be an issue if one of your children says things like:

'You always take his side,'
'I get blamed for everything,'

or even

'You love her more than you love me.'

Another giveaway is one of your children saying, 'But if you like us all the same . . .

. . . why does he get away with things?'
. . . why do you always blame me?'
. . . why do you spend more time with her?'
. . . why are you always laughing and joking with him?'

Your other child may wonder: is it because he has more interesting things to say, or she's cleverer than me and always has the right answer? Parents have to observe their own behaviour very closely to notice these more subtle things which children often don't complain about directly but are nonetheless affected by.

Favouritism? Who, Me?

It's difficult, but listen to the complaints and ask yourself whether there might be some truth in them. Do you spend more time with one child? Do you feel a special bond with one? It may be hard to accept, but recognising the truth is the first step towards doing something about it.

What You Feel and What You Do

You can't change the way you feel but you can change the way you act on those feelings. If you're honest enough – and brave enough – to admit your feelings then you're in a position to protect your less-favoured child. If your behaviour is biased, take steps to be fairer in future.

Top Tip: *It's not what you feel, it's how you act.*

See It As Your Child Sees It

If you genuinely *don't* have a favourite, where do the accusations of favouritism come from? Examine your behaviour.

- Do you usually side with one in their quarrels? (The youngest, maybe?)

- Do you think one needs more help than the other? (The less academic?)
- Does one lack confidence and do you make more of an effort to acknowledge their achievements to boost them? (That's only natural, isn't it?)
- Does one of your children have the same sense of humour as you?

With the best intentions, you may be behaving differently towards one child – and that looks like favouritism to the others!

Treat Your Children Uniquely, Not Equally

Equal love is not shown as equal treatment. Some parents go to extreme lengths to show they're not favouring one over the other. They do things like carefully measuring servings, so each receives exactly the same. If one sibling has violin lessons, the other has to have them too – even if they never wanted them in the first place! In one family, the parents would tally up the receipts for Christmas presents, and if one child had more, the other would receive a cheque to make up the difference.

This is unnecessary and causes siblings to compare over increasingly trivial things. Do you really want your children counting their baked beans? If children are complaining about different treatment, acknowledge their feelings but be clear that, since each has different needs, each will be dealt with according to their needs.

Fair Enough!

If your children keep on with 'It's not fair!' remember 'fair' is loving and valuing each of your children for who and what they are. It's not making sure each gets exactly the same as the others. If you allow your children to constantly pressure you into assessing and measuring everything they get, so nobody feels hard done by, you're on a hiding to nothing. Don't do it!

Fair Play

If your kids bicker over trivial injustices like who gets more stripes in their toothpaste, don't get involved. Hey, so one of them has got an extra potato – unfair? Remember the dad who just doesn't do fair? Unfortunately, life's not always fair and your children might as well learn to cope with disappointments at home so they're prepared for life in the outside world.

The trick is to be confident that each is getting what they need, which is not the same as getting what their siblings have. In the long run, fairness comes from treating each as individual and unique personalities, and giving to them according to their *own* needs and abilities.

If one of your children says:
'He's got more custard than me!'

Don't say:
'No he hasn't. You've both got exactly the same.'

Instead, say:
'Has he? Well, if you're still hungry afterwards, you can have second helpings.'

When It's a Question of Time

If your child says you spend more time helping her brother with his homework than you spend with her, explain that the amount of time you give depends on how much help each of them needs. If she feels she needs more help, offer to give it to her.

If one of your children says:
'You've been talking to her for ages, I want you to come and talk to me now.'

Don't say:
'Okay, I'll spend some time with you now.'

Instead, say:
'Yes, I have been talking to Amy for ages. But Amy's birthday's important; there's a lot to plan and I want to give it my full attention. When I've finished, we'll be able to have a proper chat together.'

Confidence Boosters

If your children feel insecure, they're more likely to be on the lookout for preferential treatment. What should you say when one accuses you of loving the other more? If you say, 'But I love you both equally,' they may pressure you to choose or may feel you're saying that just as a fob-off.

Instead, try stressing what it is you like so much about *them* and let them understand that each is special to you in different ways. Be specific about what you like. Say something like 'No one else has your sense of humour or writes such funny poems. And who else could help me with the gardening like you do?'

Chemistry

Sometimes, the chemistry between siblings doesn't work. They just aren't the same kind of people. These resentments may never be cleared up in childhood and may last all through life.

In one family with three grown-up sisters, the youngest sister refuses to talk to the eldest and excludes her from any family celebrations. All their conversations about family business have to take place through the middle sister.

Between brothers and sisters, sometimes personality clashes make it difficult for them to get along together. You can't alter the way they react to each other, but explain how unsettling it is to the rest of the family. Ask them to sort out their disagreements and agree a workable compromise. You may have to act as referee, but trust them to do it on their own.

Light at the End of the Tunnel
If you feel the chemistry between your children is impossible, here's a story to give you hope.

I hated my sister when we were kids. Hated, loathed, and despised her. I hid cigarettes in her pocket and then grassed her up to our dad. She used to hide my homework so I'd get into trouble. We fought all the time.

It was only after she left home to go to university I realised I missed her. I was so pleased to see her when the Christmas holidays started, and I ended up spending weekends with her in the halls of residence. We're really close friends now and the only time we had a serious falling out was when we went on holiday together for two weeks – that was a bit of a disaster! I think we both get on better with a bit of room to manoeuvre!

Special Circumstances

What's 'Special'?

If average families with two-point-three children experience sibling problems, what happens in families that have something different about them? Like twins or triplets, or a child with special needs bringing his or her own demands on their parents' time and energy. How does it affect the relationship between siblings? Does it drive a wedge between them or bring them closer together?

If You Need Support, It's Out There

These are complicated issues and this chapter offers a few guidelines – that's all. There's a list of support organisations at the end of this book if you need specialist help or someone to talk to.

1 Two, Three, Four . . . or More!

You're not alone! Multiple births are on the increase – especially with the increased use of IVF. There are approximately 10,000 twins born every year in the UK, and IVF increases your likelihood of having twins to around one in five. Although the incidence of twins and triplets – even quads – is rising fast, it's still fairly unusual in the UK.

 Top Tip: Being part of a double act or a trio brings its own challenges for siblings.

After sharing the same living space for nine months, it's not surprising twins and triplets are unusually close. It's tempting to think of your children as 'the twins' or 'the triplets'. If you always lump them together, however, it's likely they'll become hyper-close or rebel to ridiculous extremes in order to better define themselves as individuals in their own right.

For example, one friend always wears her hair in a gamine-style crop. I asked if she'd ever thought about growing it. 'I couldn't possibly do that,' she said. 'My twin sister always wears her hair down to her waist.'

 Top Tip: Allow your children space to develop their own personalities.

A Person in Their Own Right

Accentuate the differences. If your kids enjoy being together, doing the same things and having the same friends – fine. If not, don't make them feel pressured to be one unit. Avoid dressing your twins and triplets in the same clothes – it may look cute, but more than likely it will be an obstacle to feeling like a person in their own right if they're concerned that they look like a music hall double act.

You may wish to consider enquiring whether your twins can be in different classes at school, so they can make their own friends and develop their own, independent social circles. If possible, give each their own bedroom and a place to keep their personal possessions.

 Top Tip: Encourage your child to say they have a twin sister or brother, rather than say, 'I'm a twin.'

Be particularly wary of labelling and comparing when your children are so close in age and ability. If your kids look the same, others outside the home will probably be doing it already, so be careful not to do it yourselves. Be ready to counteract labels within the family – your influence will be much greater than that of others.

2 'Me Too!' – Life with a 'Gifted' Sibling

In the US, the number of profoundly gifted children has risen dramatically. Being part of a family where one child is an Olympic athlete or wins a maths scholarship to Cambridge at the age of twelve can be hard work for the whole family – especially if one child feels outshone by the outstanding sibling. Living with a child who has exceptional talents can create problems for both parents and siblings.

 Top Tip: *A very bright child places additional demands on parents for time and attention. Be sure this is not given at the expense of other children in the family.*

It's a difficult balancing act for the parents of a gifted child. On the one hand they need to give their gifted child a sense of normality and not exaggerate the importance of being gifted (which may give their child an exaggerated sense of his own importance). Often, exceptionally talented children themselves reject the label 'gifted', because it makes them feel different and sets them apart from their peers. On the other hand, parents will be reluctant to hold back the gifted child merely because the younger ones may feel inadequate.

 Top Tip: *Focus on 'different', not 'better'.*

Not Only Bigger but Better Too!

Firstborn children are more likely to be recognised as 'gifted' – even including the firstborn of identical twins! This may make it difficult for the second-born, who may feel they are growing up in the shadow of their gifted sibling. Common problems with the siblings of gifted children are feelings of jealousy and resentment and a sense of inadequacy.

Sibling Fact

Siblings of gifted children are also likely to be of above average intelligence.

Having a very bright firstborn can lead parents to underestimate the abilities of the younger child through comparison. As a general rule, for all children in the family, including the gifted child, it is important to accept them for who they are, not for any special talent they have.

Me First!

If the gifted child is a later-born child who rapidly passes his older sibling, this can be particularly frustrating for the older child. Their natural sense of leadership can be severely undermined. This is a double problem for the eldest child; having once given way to a new sibling, they are now pushed further out of the limelight because they have a 'special' younger sibling. The firstborn is more prone to be jealous than other positions in the family, so this double adjustment may occasionally have quite severe effects.

 Top Tip: Pay special attention to an older child if the second-born shows special abilities.

3 Living with a Disabled Brother or Sister

When one of your children has a physical disability, learning difficulties or a chronic health problem, they are not the only ones who need special attention. When your child's brother or sister has a medical condition, he or she also will have their own special worries and needs.

The sibling relationship becomes more complicated. In *Little Women*, the March sisters treasure 'dear Beth' and take little treats and posies of flowers up to the invalid, while, if she has enough strength, she busies herself sewing mittens for the poor children outside in the snow. Of course, as any parent who has experienced it will tell you, life just isn't like that!

How Does It Feel to the Disabled Sibling?

Some common emotions are envy, frustration and resentment. Sometimes the frustrations are physical: 'Why can't I run as fast?' 'Why do I have to have these injections?' 'Why do I have to eat this when she's having chocolate mousse?'

Sometimes, especially with learning difficulties, everything is fine until the younger child begins outstripping the older child in terms of development and independence. Sometimes the disabled sibling resents being 'fussed over'. When they reach adolescence, one may begin dating and enjoying a social life outside the home while the other feels stuck in childhood and unable to make their own way in the world.

How Does It Feel to Be the Sibling of Someone with a Disability?

Having a disabled sibling is a big responsibility. As one girl said:

> All I knew was that when my mother came home from hospital, I was going to have to look after my 'special' little sister. What I didn't realise was that I was going to have to grow up overnight.

'I Used to Wish I Couldn't Walk'

It may seem strange, but many siblings harbour deep jealousy of their disabled brother or sister. 'Why don't I get any of the attention?' 'Why is the family delighted when my sister learns to write her name, when I've been getting straight As all year?'

Hospitals try to make their paediatric departments as much fun as possible. So much so that younger children sometimes grow to resent their siblings spending days 'playing with all the toys' while they are made to go to school.

Siblings of disabled children often also become protective of their parents and studiously avoid saying anything that could worry them. They may need special attention, time and close listening before they voice their anxieties and resentment. Many organisations produce specialist books and leaflets to help mums and dads explain disabilities to younger siblings. Small children may not understand the medical reasons for their sibling 'being like they are' and so it may be important to dispel confusion and fear that it may happen to them.

Top Tip: *Nothing is more frightening than the unknown. To dispel fears, explain as much as possible in understandable language.*

Raising a child with a disability can be expensive. As your children grow up, the amount of money spent on one child's special needs may trigger jealousy – especially if it's the reason why an able-bodied sibling can't have special treats.

Divided Loyalties
A disabled sibling is often embarrassing for a brother or sister, especially when they enter puberty. They may be teased by their peers about their sibling, and then feel guilty when they are torn between a fierce protectiveness of their sibling and an overwhelming desire to have a family 'like everyone else's'.

The effect on the siblings of a disabled child may be to be 'no trouble' because they feel their parents have trouble enough already. As children, siblings may suppress any inclination to be rebellious or naughty and grow up neglecting their own needs in favour of addressing those of other people. When they are older, they may put off leaving home or going to university in order to be there for the family.

Pay Attention!
An alternative approach is to become equally 'demanding'. Below is a query to raisingkids.co.uk which shows the stresses

and strains a parent faces when trying to balance the needs of one child against another.

> My eight-year-old is very jealous of her brother, who's seven. He has ADHD (Attention Deficit Hyperactivity Disorder) and Asperger's Syndrome, and demands a lot of attention. I've stopped giving him as much attention, but she's still the same. We seem to fight all the time, and we cannot be civil to each other.
>
> (courtesy: raisingkids.co.uk)

The answer tries to give the point of view of the girl and suggests some tactics for dealing with jealousy. It also makes the mother aware of her own complex feelings to both children.

> It probably seems very strange to you that your daughter could be jealous of your son, given that he has a disability which will create many difficulties for him . . .
>
> As far as she is concerned, she is losing out on the attention stakes because he is so demanding. She has learned that if she is demanding and confrontational, she gets your attention, albeit negative attention. *But* I'm sure she's not happy that you and she are fighting all the time, and would love to be on good terms with you. The way to do it is to avoid paying attention to negative behaviour and reinforce any positive behaviour you see.
>
> Is it possible you feel guilty for not giving your daughter enough attention, and are tolerating behaviour that is simply not acceptable? On the positive side, try to make time that is just 'her time'. Why not take her out for an outing some-

where where she has your undivided attention, without having to fight for it? Try an after-school class where she could have the opportunity to shine in her own right.

Your Relationship with Your Partner

Even under normal circumstances, children can put pressure on a relationship. The extra demands of coping with a disabled child can feel overwhelming. If Mum and Dad are arguing, it's upsetting and can make your children feel insecure. Your disabled child may feel guilty and your other children may blame their sibling.

 Top Tip: *If you're finding it hard to manage, seek professional help as soon as possible.*

Don't wait for things to get out of control – life is not an endurance test and there are plenty of organisations that can offer support when it's needed.

The Same, but Different

Even with a disabled child, many parenting issues will be the same as if there was no disability, and the best approach will be to tackle them in that way. The triggers may be different, however, and often unexpected. For example, a toddler may be jealous that their older sister can still wear nappies, or a physically disabled child may be viciously competitive over schoolwork.

137

Just as in any family, don't play favourites, avoid labelling any of your children, and never pit one child against another. But if you feel things are getting out of hand, look for external assistance – it's what the professionals are there for.

Wicked Stepsisters and Stepbrothers

Stepfamilies are on the Increase

It's predicted that by 2010 there will be more stepfamilies than birth families in the UK. Forty per cent of remarriages involve live-in stepchildren, and the number of children in stepfamilies has more than tripled in the past decade.

Stepfamilies have never had a good press. Look at Snow White's jealous stepmother or Cinderella and her Ugly Sisters. Fairy tales end with the triumphant child banishing the wicked interlopers. In real life, this doesn't make for happy endings.

The 'Happy Ending' is Just the Start

Modern-day stepfamilies come about for all sorts of different reasons. There are probably as many different circumstances as there are stepfamilies. Sometimes a parent has died; occasionally the mother or father has brought up the children alone before they have met a new partner; but divorce or separation is the most common cause.

Many second or third marriages bring two sets of children together, making the often enjoyable but always difficult job of learning to live together even more of a challenge.

 Top Tip: When the adults fall in love, their children often have no say in the matter!

In today's complicated family relationships, we're dealing with real people – and that's so much messier than dealing with characters on the page.

140

Once Upon a Time . . . Some Twenty-First-Century Stories

Once upon a time . . . there was a stepmother who meant well, but couldn't help favouring her own children over her stepson. Guilty, she over-compensated by buying the boy extra presents, and her own children thought she didn't love them as much as she did him.

Once upon a time . . . a recently separated mum-of-three moved her new boyfriend in with his two kids. Her children loved him, and he rapidly made the transition from 'Uncle Mike' to 'Dad'. The kids got on like a house on fire. After eighteen months, she realised that, no matter how good he was with the children, she'd made a mistake and she didn't actually love him. Rather than hurt the children and split up the new family unit, she married him as soon as her divorce came through. They divorced three years later.

Once upon a time . . . an absent father agreed to pay school fees for his children, while their stepsister had to go to the local comprehensive. Her stepsiblings called her 'pikey' and 'thicko'. She called them 'stuck up' and 'snobby toffs'. When she left home for university, they never spoke to each other again.

There are no pantomime heroes or villains in these scenarios. Sometimes it works like clockwork, sometimes it doesn't. However it works out, though, there are a lot of assumptions about stepfamilies.

Prepare the Ground

Stepsiblings' relationships are deeply affected by the way their parents handle their own relationships. If you can manage it, some preparation beforehand will certainly help. Of course, this being the real world, this is not always possible, but it will help if you think about how you want your new stepfamily to work and consider some of your own assumptions about stepfamilies in advance. Talk things through with your partner beforehand too (and with your ex, if you can). If you anticipate possible problem areas, you can try and work them out before they become too tricky.

The More the Merrier?

In a first marriage, the biggest challenge is working out how two people can get along together. In subsequent relationships, the number of people involved can be three, four, five or more – plus part-time members, previous partners, and entire sets of grandparents and other relatives.

 Top Tip: *Be realistic in your expectations of how your children will get along. Siblings who have lived together all their lives can still fight like cat and dog, so don't expect more of stepsiblings.*

Remember, too, that living apart and living together are two quite different kettles of fish – the latter requiring far more negotiation and flexibility than the first. The more personalities which have to be contained within the new relationship, the more difficult it can be. The presence of pre-teens or teens who have their own life crises to deal with can complicate relationships still further.

'We Don't Do It Like That!'

Moving in together may be what you've always wanted, but be prepared for it to bring new problems. Your stepfamily can create its own way of living together, but it will take time. The way you work together will be different from when you did it the first time round. Realistic expectations from the outset will help everyone to work together to achieve a level of harmony. It's tempting to believe that stepfamilies who live apart will get along better than those living under the same roof, because they can get away from each other. In fact, the opposite is more likely to be true. Constant comings and goings make it harder

to establish family rules and routines. If people are together every day, they have a much better chance of working things out.

Why Do They Fight?

In stepfamilies, the stresses of ordinary family life are multiplied, especially in the early days. A new stepbrother or sister can be seen as an invader, especially if they move into the family home. Stepsiblings come together with different expectations, family habits and rules. Jealousy can erupt over issues of space, possessions, age differences and the inevitable rivalry for parents' love. Until a new way of living together develops, these conflicts are almost inevitable.

'They're Young, They'll Adapt Quickly'

This may be partly true, but it's just as likely that, having had limited choice in the decision about the new set-up, your children will also have a limited vested interest in making it work. Sharing a home and parents is difficult enough for natural brothers and sisters, but it's even more of a challenge for stepsiblings who have extra obstacles to overcome. Some conflict and complaint is inevitable.

It is probably true that the younger the children are, the more likely they are to come to terms with their changed situation. Older children will often have developed an especially close relationship with their sole parent and may take more time to adjust to their new extended family.

Is Love All You Need?

Despite even the best intentions, it's unlikely that a step-parent will feel the same towards their stepchildren as they feel towards their own children. The feeling is probably mutual. Any step-parent who has been told, 'You're not my mum/dad, I don't have to do what you say!' knows this for themselves.

But if you and your partner love each other enough, will the problems disappear? Your own relationship can provide the basis of a successful new family but it shouldn't blind you as a couple to the issues the whole family is likely to face. It's only understandable that you should want to spend time alone with your partner and to physically express your affection for each other, but be careful not to do it to the exclusion of your children.

Many families do make it work, but the hard work involved cannot be underestimated and the notion that all members will grow to love each other effortlessly is a total fairy story. If things are difficult, first work towards the more realistic and achievable aim of mutual tolerance, which will grant everyone involved a bit of breathing space from which (who knows?) a more positive relationship may develop.

Laying Foundations

In an earlier chapter we looked at ways to prepare your child for a new baby brother or sister. Preparing them to become part of a stepfamily is a similar process. There are a few key things to bear in mind, especially if both sets of children are older:

- Give them time to get used to the idea.
- Give them time to meet and get to know each other.
- Give them time to get used to each other alone and on their own terms, with minimum adult supervision.
- Recognise the territorial feelings associated with stepsiblings moving into the home. Anyone (uninvited by you) moving into your living space can pose a threat. Although it's not an option for many of us, some parents have even taken the decision to move into an entirely new house or flat in order to establish their newly constituted family. It's new territory for everybody. No one is an interloper and no one has to give up their bedroom or wardrobe space. If it's a practical option, it's worth considering.
- Lay down house rules from the very beginning – what's shared, what's private, what's acceptable and what isn't. Both parents need to be consistent – if Mum insists on children helping in the kitchen and Dad doesn't, decide what the house policy will be before confusion and resentment set in. You can't have one set of children helping while the others watch television.
- Work together to make it a success. Even if you disagree with what your partner says and does on a particular issue, don't make too much of it in front of the children. Wait until you have time to discuss it alone; then make a policy, announce it and stick to it.

When They Just Don't Get On

Don't assume it's your fault when you and a new partner have steadily worked hard to build an emotional bond but the children from your two households haven't exactly fallen in love with each other! The closeness a shared household demands will have come suddenly for them and will inevitably require a fair amount of adjustment, so give them the time and space they need.

> **Top Tip:** *All children fight with their siblings at some point but, in the short term at least, the likelihood of arguments goes sky-high when stepsiblings are involved.*

Stepsiblings of All Ages Will Fight

If your kids are teenagers, conflict is even more likely. Teenagers have busy lives and a growing burden of responsibilities. Built-up tension must be released, and this often happens at home – after all, making a fool of yourself in front of your family is far better than looking a right muppet in front of your mates. A stepsibling – the resident enemy – is an easy target for attack in these situations.

Accept that Your Children May Not Love Their Stepsiblings

Early on, it's important to appreciate that though you may have chosen your partner, your children did not choose your partner's kids. Don't necessarily expect them to become as close as 'real' brothers and sisters, but concentrate instead on finding ways to help them co-exist peacefully and give the relationships a chance to grow.

Working Out a Truce

Take time to listen to both sides of any disagreements, not just your own child's version of things. When you think you've understood what's at the bottom of their (probably mutual) dislike, call a family meeting to discuss the situation.

The most important thing here is to ban all name-calling, criticising and other negative behaviour. Insist that, since they live under the same roof, it's vital for everyone's sanity that they find a workable way of living together.

 Top Tip: *Get them to list the main causes of friction, then ask them to choose the two or three most common flashpoints and to work out possible ways of diffusing the situations.*

Don't Let Your Children's Conflicts Sabotage Your Relationship

Despite your natural inclinations, you and your partner must at all costs avoid getting drawn into the conflict. Though you may act as impartial referees, it's important that the onus remains with them to resolve their differences.

How I Learned to Stop Fighting and Love My Brother

Some Tricks of the Trade

When rivalry between brothers and sisters begins to disturb the whole family, at some point something has to be done about it. The question is, what?

What positive steps can parents take to restore peace and help their children get along better? Better still, how can mums and dads help their children build bonds that will last for life? There are four key principles that parents can adopt to make things better:

1   understand what lies behind the conflict;
2   acknowledge the feelings involved;

3   encourage your children to express their feelings constructively;
4   value each child for themselves.

1 Understand What Lies Behind the Conflict

Listen and Learn

If you want to know what lies beneath all the conflict, the first thing is to listen. Pay close attention to what they are saying: you will get an insight into what is bothering one or both of them.

'You always take her side. You always blame me!'
'You never spend time helping me with my painting.'

Notice the key words 'always' and 'never'. It's the kind of thing kids say all the time, isn't it? Yes it is, but . . . is it normally one particular child who says it? Do they say it a lot? In these situations, it's important to ask yourself whether there may be something in it. *Do* you take his side more than is fair? *Do* you blame her more than you should?

Heard It All Before?

Try to avoid the temptation of assuming that you already know what is going on. In a group as intimate as a family, it's easy to think you know what makes your children tick. You may think this one is inclined to be bossy, that one gives in too easily, etc., and make your judgements accordingly. You might suppose you know what your child thinks – or should think – but you could be missing important information.

When I was a child my older sister was always picking on me. In my family, we were always teasing each other and, as the youngest, I seemed to be the butt of most of the jokes. If it was funny it didn't matter how unkind it was, you were just supposed to laugh. I really hated it and sometimes my sister was really cruel with her teasing, but my family just thought I was being a wimp and over-reacting. They would say, 'Where's your sense of humour?' Funny wasn't always funny to me. When I said, 'Make her stop!' I just wish someone had listened to me instead of saying, 'Oh, don't be so sensitive, she's only joking.'

This girl would have liked a chance to say that, though the teasing may have seemed funny to others, more often it was hurtful to her and she would have liked it to stop. As it was, left unchecked – encouraged, even – it undermined the self-confidence of the younger girl and encouraged the surreptitious bullying of the older one.

2 Acknowledge the Feelings Involved

What if you feel the issues go deeper than day-to-day spats about who gets first go on the Playstation or who has the most fish fingers?

Once again, listening is vital: pay attention, acknowledge what's being said and name the feeling. Don't jump in with

- your own opinions ('I don't think she really means it');

- your own solutions ('Why don't you just walk away?');
- your own criticisms ('Don't be so touchy').

Name that Feeling

Simply listening and acknowledging the feeling is a surprisingly powerful tool. Indeed, you may be surprised at the feeling you are naming. If the parents of the teased younger sister had named her feelings, they might not have been so quick to dismiss them.

Suppose they had said something like, 'It sounds as if you are feeling very hurt about what your sister said.' It may be that they would have decided to limit the teasing, because now they saw it not as 'funny' but as 'hurtful'.

Top Tip: If you want to encourage your child to talk about their feelings, be attentive and be ready to listen when they want to talk – not just when it's convenient.

You may think you'll fuel the feeling by recognising it, but the opposite is true. By acknowledging the feeling – especially if it's one of the 'bad' ones like envy, anger or resentment – you'll be letting your child know it's okay to feel like that. Instead of brushing things under the carpet, they can be brought out into the open where you can deal with them. Remember how Dracula crumbles to dust when the sunlight hits him? You can zap many hidden problems in the same way.

3 Encourage Your Children to Act Constructively

By listening properly, you can encourage your children to confront their own worries and feelings. This helps them on the way to understanding their own emotions and developing emotional intelligence – in other words, growing up!

 Top Tip: *The first step in dealing with a worry is being able to bring it out into the open.*

From this point, you can help your child face the problem and perhaps find a solution to it.

It's Okay to Feel It but Don't Act On It

Recognising the feelings and expressing them verbally is fine and helps relieve tension. You can't do anything about the way your child feels but you can make it clear there are limits on how they express those feelings. For example, it's fine for your child to feel angry because his little sister tore his homework book, but it's emphatically *not* fine for him to smack her.

Assertive, Not Aggressive

Teach your children skills for dealing with sibling conflicts, and in your own behaviour towards them model those skills yourself. They can learn to stand up for themselves and express their anger without hitting or being verbally abusive.

Teach them to say what it is they don't like in a firm and forceful way rather than name-calling. Your children can learn to say something along the lines of 'I don't like it when you go crying to Mum every time you don't get your own way,' instead of 'You're a such a wimp and a cry-baby! . . . and a bed wetter!!'

> **Top Tip:** *In solving conflict, as in everything else, remember that you're a role model – like it or not!*

Find a Fix, Not a Fight

Throughout this book we have stressed the importance of making brothers and sisters take responsibility for sorting out their problems. For example: 'You've dirtied the dress you borrowed without asking. What are you going to do about it?'

When this happened with a friend's teenage daughters recently, I expected bloodshed. To my surprise, after an (admittedly heated) discussion, little sister stalked off to the local dry cleaner with the jam-stained frock. I asked the elder sister how she did it. 'I wanted Mel to get my dress *clean* again, not waste time fighting about it. She'll think twice about borrowing my things next time – that dry cleaning's going to cost half her pocket money!'

Big sister was obviously furious, though. I asked her why she'd kept so much self-control. 'I know if I'd have slapped her, we'd both have been in the wrong. She knew she was out of order – it was better to work out a way for Mel to make it up to me without her feeling humiliated.'

Top Tip: *Teach your children they should learn to look for a solution – not a fight.*

In encouraging your children to act constructively, it's important to emphasise the importance of the warring parties meeting halfway. The person who is angry has the responsibility of withholding her anger and behaving calmly. The offender is also obliged to behave constructively and not walk away from the problem he caused. Both sides may take a fair bit of convincing!

If it's a recurrent problem, once the fighting and rowing has subsided take your children aside and ask them to sort the issue out once and for all. Generally, withholding a privilege or threatening a penalty is enough to concentrate their minds and they can work together to find a solution. Praise them when (and if!) they show signs of progress.

Family Meeting

Where there are major issues that worry parents and begin to disrupt the family, then calling a family meeting to discuss the matter may be a solution. Below are some generally agreed guidelines for running a family meeting.

- Agree the rules: no name-calling, no shouting, no interrupting.
- State the problem in a way that everyone can agree with.
- Brainstorm solutions and list them without commenting.

- Discuss each of the options.
- Discuss how the solution will be implemented.

Here's an example of how such a meeting might go. The problem is that two brothers share a bedroom. It's quite a large room and each has enough space for his needs. The problem arises over music; each loathes the other's musical taste and neither wants the other to play his music in their room. Since each likes to play music throughout the day and the other can't avoid it, every day two or three fights erupt between them. It

158

begins to disrupt the whole household. Finally a family meeting is called and rules agreed.

Solutions brainstormed include the following, which (in theory) are listed without comment or discussion:

- a rota, so each has an agreed time when he can play his music;
- one brother to move his hi-fi equipment to the basement;
- headphones;
- whoever starts first has priority for an hour.

The pros and cons of each are then discussed until the brothers agree the solution they think is best. The way in which the solution is carried out is then discussed. In the real-life situation, the boys decided to have no music at all if either of them was doing homework, and to take it in turns on alternate days once the homework was finished.

4 Value Each Child for Themselves

Watch Yourself!
When a parent takes a great deal of pride in the qualities of one of their children, it can often stoke the flames of jealousy in other children in the family. What each and every child (and adult) wants is to feel loved and valued for who they are, not to feel 'second-best' or less valued when compared to their brother or sister.

It's so important that we love our children for who they are – celebrating differences, but demonstrating our love equally.

It's not always as straightforward as we'd like to think. For example, this is the experience of one mother with a very clever daughter and an older boy of average ability.

> I knew he was envious of her quickness and brains, so I was careful not to speak too much about her achievements in front of him. If we had visitors and they asked how she was doing in school, I tended to play things down. It was my husband who pointed out to me more subtle signs that I was completely unaware of. He pointed out that when we were out together, I tended to point things out to her rather than my son. If he gave his opinion on something, I didn't listen with the same attention as when she spoke. He also accused me of asking her difficult questions, just so I could 'marvel at her cleverness' (his words). I felt terrible. I just didn't notice myself doing these things.

What Every Child Wants

Like adults, children want to be valued for themselves and have their unique and special qualities recognised and acknowledged. Parents should ask themselves, 'What makes my child who he is?' His qualities may be things you take for granted, like having a terrific sense of humour or the ability to make friends. Practical skills like cookery, organisational abilities, being a sympathetic listener or keeping people entertained, are all talents to be built on and made their own.

A good parent reflects back to a child a sense of their own uniqueness and specialness. Where each child feels valued for themselves they are unlikely to resent or be envious of their siblings' abilities.

Building Bonds

Growing Together

To build strong relationships between brothers and sisters in the family there are three things parents can do. These can be summarised under the headings

- what we say;
- what we do;
- what we celebrate.

1 What We Say

Family Matters
It's difficult to speak about sibling relationships outside the context of the whole family. If the family ties are strong, then

sibling relationships are also likely to be strong. Make family life a priority and members of the family will feel bonded with each other.

Don't be afraid to tell your children that brothers and sisters are important to each other, that blood is thicker than water. In some societies, the kinship of brother and sister is celebrated symbolically. In India, once a year a sister ties her brother's hand to her own for a whole day, symbolically highlighting their importance to each other.

Siblings are for Life!

In the UK, we have no confirming rituals like this. We have to make sure that our children get the message about how important they are to each other. Use any opportunity to tell them that this is an important, life-long relationship for them.

A friend of mine gave me an example from her own family of how she emphasised to her children the importance of not taking each other for granted.

At dinner, Jenna asked her older sister to please cut her a slice of bread. Her sister's response was really rude and offhand. She thrust the bread at her, saying, 'Cut it yourself!' I was furious. I told her that she wouldn't speak to a complete stranger like that, and how could she speak to her own sister like that.

One for All and All for One
Families work best when they stick together and recognise their responsibility for each other. This includes brothers and sisters. At school, older children are often exhorted to 'keep an eye on your little brother or sister'. Even very young children can learn early on that 'we all pull together and when things have to be done, everybody pitches in'.

2 What We Do

Doing fun things together makes everyone feel good about each other. This is easier said than done, since modern life often limits the number of things families do together. Microwaves and ready-made food mean family members don't have to eat together. A large majority of seven-year-olds have a television in their room and watch alone. After-school activities take one child in one direction and his brother or sister in another.

Spending time together, even in the same house, now requires special planning.

 Top Tip: *Increase the amount of time the family spends together and increase bonds that bind.*

Eat Together

Eat together and recap the day, so brothers and sisters can stay in touch with each other's lives. A report in the UK revealed that only one in three children had eaten a meal with their family in the previous week. Eating together is one of the most essential and basic activities a family can undertake. It is an opportunity to talk together, to share the day's activities with other family members, to have fun, to laugh and if needs be to help each other.

Work Together

Even the chores can be an opportunity for time spent together. Rather than dividing the chores, share them. After Sunday lunch, my three children were left to do the washing up. They put on the radio with their favourite station and they fooled around and laughed together while they worked. They don't like the washing up – who does? – but together they made the best of a bad job.

The Family that Plays Together Stays Together

Leisure is a place where activities and shared interests can be expressed. Take your children swimming, playing tennis, to the cinema, to visit friends, to museums, to play football – whatever it is that interests you, share it with other members of your family. Try to choose activities everyone can join in.

Watch Together

Even watching television together can also be a source of communication and sharing. Watch as a family. Let the children watch together, and when possible watch with them. Asked for one of his favourite memories of childhood, this boy recalled Friday evenings at home.

Friday was comedy night. We didn't have to get up for school next day so we were allowed to stay up late. We always had a nice dinner together and then we would all watch TV. Someone would make tea, we would have a nice cake and settle down to watch two hours of comedy. Even as a teenager, I looked forward to Fridays with the family.

 Top Tip: Don't have one television per child.

167

3 What We Celebrate

Celebrations are ways of showing what's important to families. Celebrating a birthday makes a child feel special and connected to other people. For that day, one child is centre stage and, perhaps more than at any other time, his parents and brothers and sisters can show how much they love him. Encourage that feeling of being able to do something for one of your brothers and sisters, as opposed to the usual bickering and squabbling.

Expect the best of your children, not the worst, when it comes to their feelings about their siblings. In a previous chapter I mentioned my friend Lizzie, who gave each of her four

168

children presents when one of them had a birthday. Why should they have presents? It's not their birthday. It's as if she is saying her other children can't enjoy their sibling's pleasure without feeling resentful. Rather than pandering to their feelings, Lizzie should encourage her other three children to take pleasure in making their sibling's day a special one. She could have encouraged them to make a card or prepare a special present.

Your Success is My Success

When one child achieves something, encourage his brothers and sisters to share it.

If your teenager is showing her GCSE artwork at school, take the whole family along to view it. If your seven-year-old is entered into a swimming gala, make sure it's not only his parents who turn up to cheer him on but his brothers and sisters too.

 Top Tip: *There is an alternative to rivalry! Help them build bonds now and they will reap the rewards throughout their lives.*

If each child feels valued for herself and knows she has special qualities that are appreciated, she is unlikely to feel envious. She can show wholehearted pleasure in her siblings' achievements.

Am I My Brother's Keeper? Yes! And My Sister's Too!

The sibling relationship is an emotional roller-coaster, warm and close one minute and battling the next. There's so much more to sibling relationships than rivalry and jealousy. Throughout this book we wanted to show what strengths there are in the sibling bond and how much learning and support children can take from their brothers and sisters. We wanted, too, to highlight the role that parents can play in reinforcing the ties that bind brothers and sisters together in an enduring life-long relationship.

When we began, we looked at all the great things that brothers and sisters bring to each other. In that vein, perhaps we should end with something a friend said when he heard we were writing a book about siblings and their relationships.

People say you can't choose your family but you can choose your friends. I couldn't have chosen a better friend than my sister.

Further Information

Organisations

Parentalk
PO Box 23142
London SE1 0ZT

Tel: 020 7450 9073
Fax: 020 7450 9060
e-mail: info@parentalk.co.uk
Web site: www.parentalk.co.uk

Provides a range of resources and services designed to inspire parents to enjoy parenthood.

Web site: www.parentalkatwork.co.uk

A new web site for parents wanting to strike a healthy balance between work and family life. Parentalk at Work provides top tips, practical advice, discussion forums and links to other organisations.

www.raisingkids.co.uk

Individual advice from Dr Pat Spungin and other qualified experts, a huge reference library of parenting solutions, plus online discussions for support from the raisingkids.co.uk online community of parents in similar situations.

Care for the Family
PO Box 488
Cardiff CF15 7YY

Tel: 029 2081 0800
Fax: 029 2081 4089
e-mail:
    care.for.the.family@cff.org.uk
Web site:
    www.care-for-the-family.org.uk

Provides support for families through seminars, resources and special projects.

Child Benefit Centre
Waterview Park
Pattenson Industrial Estate
Washington
Tyne and Wear NE38 8QA

Tel: 08701 555540
e-mail:
　childbenefit@mso4.dss.gov.uk
Web site: www.dss.gov.uk

Administers all child benefit claims.

Child Support Agency
PO Box 55
Brierley Hill
West Midlands DY5 1YL
Tel: 08457 133133 (enquiry line)

In Northern Ireland:
Great Northern Tower
17 Great Victoria Street
Belfast BT2 7AD
Tel: 028 9089 6896

The Government agency that assesses maintenance levels for parents who no longer live with their children.

Children 1st
41 Polwarth Terrace
Edinburgh EH11 1NU

Tel: 0131 337 8539
Fax: 0131 346 8284
e-mail: children1st@zetnet.co.uk

A national Scottish voluntary organisation providing advice and support to parents on the care and protection of their children.

Contact-A-Family
209–211 City Road
London EC1V 1JN

Helpline: 0808 808 3555
Tel: 020 7608 8700
Fax: 020 7608 8701
e-mail: info@cafamily.org.uk
Web site: www.cafamily.org.uk

Brings together families whose children have disabilities.

Council for Disabled Children
8 Wakley Street
London EC1V 7QE

Tel: 020 7843 6061/6058
Fax: 020 7278 9512
e-mail: jkhan@ncb.org.uk
Web site: www.ncb.org.uk

Provides an information and advice service on all matters relating to disability for children and their families.

Couple Counselling Scotland
105 Handover Street
Edinburgh EH2 1DJ

Tel: 0131 225 5006

Provides a confidential counselling service for relationship problems of any kind.

Dads & Lads

YMCA England National Dads & Lads Project
Dee Bridge House
25–27 Lower Bridge Street
Chester CH1 1RS

Tel: 01244 403090
e-mail: dirk@parenting.ymca.org.uk
ahowie@themail.co.uk

Locally based projects run jointly by YMCA and Care for the Family for fathers and sons, mentors and boys. They offer a unique opportunity to get together with other fathers and sons for a game of football and other activities. To find out where your nearest Dads & Lads project is based or to get help starting a new one, please contact Dirk Uitterdijk at the above address.

Fathers Direct

Tamarisk House
37 The Tele Village
Crickhowell
Powys NP8 1BP

Tel: 01873 810515
Web site: www.fathersdirect.com

An information resource for fathers.

Gingerbread

16–17 Clerkenwell Close
London EC1R 0AA

Tel: 020 7336 8183
Fax: 020 7336 8185
e-mail: office@gingerbread.org.uk
Web site: www.gingerbread.org.uk

Provides day-to-day support and practical help for lone parents.

Health Development Agency

30 Great Peter Street
London SW1P 2HW

Publications: 01235 465565
Tel: 020 7222 5300
Fax: 020 7413 8900
Web site: www.hda-online.org.uk

Produces a wide range of leaflets and other useful information on a variety of topics for families.

Home-Start UK

2 Salisbury Road
Leicester LE1 7QR

Tel: 0116 233 9955
Fax: 0116 233 0232
e-mail: info@home-start.org.uk
Web site: www.home-start.org.uk

In Northern Ireland:
133 Bloomfield Avenue
Belfast BT5

Tel/fax: 028 9046 0772

*Volunteers offer support, friendship
and practical help to young families
in their own homes.*

Meet-A-Mum Association (MAMA)
26 Avenue Road
London SE25 4DX

Helpline: 020 8768 0123
 (Mon–Fri 7–10 p.m.)
Tel: 01761 433598
e-mail: meet-a-mum.assoc@blue
 yonder.co.uk
Web site: www.mama.org.uk

*Provides counselling, practical
support and group therapy for
women suffering from post-natal
depression.*

**National Association for Maternal and Child
Welfare**
40–42 Osnaburgh Street
London NW1 3ND

Tel: 020 7383 4117

*Telephone advice on childcare and
family life.*

The National Autistic Society
393 City Road
London EC1V 1NG

Autism helpline: 020 7903 3555
 (Mon–Fri 10 a.m.–4 p.m.)
Parent to Parent: 0800 9520 520
 (your call is logged on an answer-
 phone and the relevant regional
 volunteer calls you back)
Tel: 0870 600 8585
e-mail: autismhelpline@nas.org.uk
Web site: www.oneworld.org/
 autism-uk

National Childminding Association
8 Masons Hill
Bromley
Kent BR2 9EY

Advice line: 0800 169 4486 (Mon,
 Tues & Thurs 10 a.m.–12 &
 2–4 p.m.; Fri 2–4 p.m.)
Tel: 020 8464 6164
Fax: 020 8290 6834
e-mail: info@ncma.org.uk
Web site: www.ncma.org.uk

*Informs childminders, parents and
employers about the best practice in
childminding.*

National Council for One Parent Families
255 Kentish Town Road
London NW5 2LX

Lone Parent Line: 0800 018 5026
Maintenance & Money Line: 020

7428 5424 (Mon & Fri 10.30
a.m.–1.30 p.m.; Wed 3–6 p.m.)
Web site:
www.oneparentfamilies.org.uk

*An information service for lone
parents.*

National Eczema Society
Hill House
Highgate Hill
London N19 5NA

Information line: 0870 241 3604
(weekdays 1–4 p.m.)
General enquiries: 020 7281 3553
Web site: www.eczema.org

*The National Eczema Society is the
only charity in the UK dedicated to
providing support and information
for people with eczema and their
carers.*

National Family and Parenting Institute
430 Highgate Studios
53–79 Highgate Road
London NW5 1TL

Tel: 020 7424 3460
Fax: 020 7485 3590
e-mail: info@nfpi.org
Web site: www.nfpi.org

*An independent charity set up to
provide a strong national focus on
parenting and families in the twenty-
first century.*

**National NEWPIN (New Parent and Infant
Network)**
Sutherland House
35 Sutherland Square
Walworth
London SE17 3EE

Tel: 020 7703 6326
Fax: 020 7701 2660
e-mail: quality@nationalnewpin.
    freeserve.co.uk
Web site: www.newpin.org.uk

*A network of local centres offering a
range of services for parents and
children.*

NHS Direct
Advice line: 0845 4647
Web site: www.nhsdirect.co.uk

NHS Smoking Quitline
Helpline: 0800 169 0169
Web site:
    www.giveupsmoking.co.uk

NIPPA (The early years organisation)
6C Wildflower Way
Belfast BT12 6TA

Tel: 028 9066 2825
Fax: 028 9038 1270
e-mail: mail@nippa.org
Web site: www.nippa.org

*Promotes high-quality early child-
hood care and education services.*

NSPCC

NSPCC National Centre
42 Curtain Road
London EC2A 3NH

Helpline: 0800 800 5000
Tel: 020 7825 2500
Fax: 020 7825 2525
Web site: www.nspcc.org.uk

Aims to prevent child abuse and neglect in all its forms and give practical help to families with children at risk. The NSPCC also produces leaflets with information and advice on positive parenting – for these, call 020 7825 2500.

One Parent Families Scotland

13 Gayfield Square
Edinburgh EH1 3NX

Tel: 0131 556 3899/4563
Fax: 0131 557 9650
e-mail: opfs@gn.apc.org
Web site: www.gn.apc.org/opfs

Provides information, training, counselling and support to one-parent families throughout Scotland.

Oneplusone

The Wells
7/15 Rosebery Avenue
London EC1R 4SP

Tel: 020 7841 3660
Fax: 020 7841 3670

e-mail: info@oneplusone.org.uk
Web site: www.oneplusone.org.uk

Aims to build through research a framework for understanding contemporary marriage and partnership.

Parenting Education & Support Forum

Unit 431 Highgate Studios
53–79 Highgate Road
London NW5 1TL

Tel: 020 7284 8370
Fax: 020 7485 3587
e-mail: pesf@dial.pipex.com
Web site:
   www.parenting-forum.org.uk

Aims to raise awareness of the importance of parenting and its impact on all aspects of child development.

Parentline Plus

520 Highgate Studios
53–76 Highgate Road
Kentish Town
London NW5 1TL

Helpline: 0808 800 2222
Textphone: 0800 783 6783
Fax: 020 7284 5501
e-mail: centraloffice@parentline
   plus.org.uk
Web site:
   www.parentlineplus.org.uk

Provides a freephone helpline called

Parentline and courses for parents via the Parent Network Service. Parentline Plus also includes the National Stepfamily Association. For all information, call the Parentline freephone number: 0808 800 2222.

Parents Advice Centre
Floor 4
Franklin House
12 Brunswick Street
Belfast BT2 7GE

Helpline: 028 9023 8800
e-mail: belfast@pachelp.org
Web site: www.pachelp.org

Parents Anonymous
6–9 Manor Gardens
London N7 6LA

Tel: 020 7263 8918 (Mon–Fri)

24-hour answering service for parents who feel they can't cope or feel they might abuse their children.

Parents at Work
45 Beech Street
London EC2Y 8AD

Tel: 020 7628 3565
Fax: 020 7628 3591
e-mail: info@parentsatwork.org.uk
Web site:
www.parentsatwork.org.uk

Provides advice and information about childcare provision.

Positive Parenting
1st Floor
2A South Street
Gosport PO12 1ES

Tel: 023 9252 8787
Fax: 023 9250 1111
e-mail: info@parenting.org.uk
Web site: www.parenting.org.uk

Aims to prepare people for the role of parenting by helping parents, those about to become parents and also those who lead parenting groups.

Relate
Herbert Gray College
Little Church Street
Rugby CV21 3AP
Tel: 01788 573241
e-mail:
enquiries@national.relate.org.uk
Web site: www.relate.org.uk

In Northern Ireland:
76 Dublin Road
Belfast BT2 7HP
Tel: 028 9032 3454

Provides a confidential counselling service for relationship problems of any kind. Local branches are listed in the phone book.

Twins and Multiple Birth Association (TAMBA)
Harnott House
309 Chester Road
Ellesmere Port
Cheshire CH66 1QQ

Helpline: 01732 868000 (Mon–Fri
  7–11 p.m.; Sat & Sun 10 a.m.–
  11 p.m.)

Tel: 08701 214000
e-mail: enquiries@tambahq.org.uk
Web site: www.tamba.org.uk

Provides information and support to families with twins, triplet sand more.

Parenting Courses

- **Parentalk Parenting Course**
  A new parenting course designed to give parents the opportunity to share their experiences, learn from each other and discover some principles of parenting. For more information, phone 0700 2000 500.

- **Positive Parenting**
  Publishes a range of low-cost, easy-to-read, common-sense resource materials which provide help, information and advice. Responsible for running a range of parenting courses across the UK. For more information, phone 023 9252 8787.

- **Parent Network**
  For more information, call Parentline Plus on 0808 800 2222.

The **Paren**talk Parenting Course

Helping you to be a Better Parent

Being a parent is not easy. **Parentalk** is a new, video-led, parenting course designed to give groups of parents the opportunity to share their experiences, learn from each other and discover some principles of parenting. It is suitable for anyone who is a parent or is planning to become a parent.

The Parentalk Parenting Course features:

Steve Chalke – TV Presenter; author on parenting and family issues; father of four and **Parentalk** Chairman.
Rob Parsons – author of *The Sixty Minute Father* and *The Sixty Minute Mother*; and Executive Director of Care for the Family.
Dr Caroline Dickinson – inner city-based GP and specialist in obstetrics, gynaecology and paediatrics.
Kate Robbins – well-known actress and comedienne.

Each **Parentalk** session is packed with group activities and discussion starters.

Made up of eight sessions, the **Parentalk** Parenting Course is easy to use and includes everything you need to host a group of up to ten parents.

Each Parentalk Course Pack contains:
- A **Parentalk** video
- Extensive, easy-to-use, group leader's guide
- Ten copies of the full-colour course material for members
- Photocopiable sheets/OHP masters

Price £49.95

Additional participant materials are available so that the course can be run again and again.

To order your copy, or to find out more, please contact:

Parentalk

PO Box 23142, London SE1 0ZT
Tel: 020 7450 9073
Fax: 020 7450 9060
e-mail: info@parentalk.co.uk